The Study of Judaism

The Study of Judaism

Authenticity, Identity, Scholarship

Aaron W. Hughes

Published by State University of New York Press, Albany

For information, contact State University of New York Press, Albany, NY
www.sunypress.edu

Production by Jenn Bennett
Marketing by Michael Campochiaro

Library of Congress Cataloging-in-Publication Data

Hughes, Aaron W., date
  The study of Judaism : authenticity, identity, scholarship /
Aaron W. Hughes.
       pages cm
  Includes bibliographical references and index.
  ISBN 978-1-4384-4861-9 (hardcover : alk. paper)
  ISBN 978-1-4384-4862-6 (pbk. : alk. paper)
  1. Judaism.   I. Title.
  BM45.H84 2013
  296.071—dc23   2012049545

10 9 8 7 6 5 4 3 2 1

To the loving memory of my father
William Hughes
(April 11, 1927–June 2, 2013)

Contents

Acknowledgments

This volume owes its genesis to a set of issues and methodologies supplied by my colleagues in the North American Association for the Study of Religion (NAASR). Often critical of the status quo, this organization's *raison d'être* is the investigation of that which brings data constructed as "religious" into existence. The focus, in other words, is on what is commonly called "metastudies." I would accordingly like to thank my colleagues in that organization for their patience and good humor: William E. Arnal, Herbert Berg, Willi Braun, Matthew Day, Craig Martin, Russell McCutcheon, and Donald Wiebe. I also owe a debt of gratitude to my colleagues working in Jewish Studies who are sympathetic to my argument and have offered encouragement: Zachary Braiterman, Sergey Dolgopolski, Jeremiah Haber, Dana Hollander, Martin Kavka, Shaul Magid, Randi Rashkover, and Elliot R. Wolfson.

Finally, I would like to thank Jennifer Hall for her constant support and companionship. Her patience in talking things through, both intellectual and otherwise, means a tremendous amount to me. I am also grateful to senior acquisitions editor Nancy Ellegate at SUNY Press for her encouragement and for seeing this project through to the light of day.

Introduction

In 2007 I published a slim and what I hoped would be a provocative volume entitled *Situating Islam: The Past and Future of an Academic Discipline*. This work functioned as a genealogical and analytic exploration of the study of the study of Islam. What, for example, are the various assumptions, ideological agendas, and political implications involved in those who have studied and continue to study Islam professionally? These manifold processes, I argued, are what ultimately make the discipline—its written and unwritten rules—possible. Russell McCutcheon, the editor of the series in which that book appeared, encouraged me at the time to try to do something similar for Jewish studies, my other and primary disciplinary home. His exposure to Jewish studies had been primarily negative, thinking—not incorrectly—that Jewish studies tended to be peopled largely by Jews who studied their own religious tradition in a rather self-congratulatory and apologetic manner. The result, according to him, is that Jewish studies has largely established itself as a fortified ethnic enclave within larger departments of religious studies, becoming, as it were, a problematic subfield within a larger and equally problematic discipline.

For the past five years I have thought extensively about his assessment of the field. My natural reaction was to argue with him, to make the case that Jewish studies was a healthy discipline that studied, analyzed, quantified, and qualified data from the length and breadth of Jewish history (spanning from ca. 1000 BCE to the present). In the meantime, a number of conversations happened that led me to question some of my own assumptions. I recall being early for a panel at the Annual Meeting of the Association for Jewish Studies (AJS) and finding myself part of a conversation in which the panelists and some audience members—all roughly my own age—reminisced about the same Jewish summer camp they used to go to—their shared

1

songs, counselors, and so on. Having grown up in a non-Jewish environment, I felt uncomfortable and unable (and unwilling) to enter
their conversation of "Jewish geography" (i.e., who knows whom or
is related to whom). Several months later, I was having lunch with
a friend and fellow non-Muslim Islamicist, and for some reason, our
conversation turned to whether he had ever thought of moving institutions. He informed me that he had, but that he now worried that
Islamic studies was becoming too much like Jewish studies in the
sense that soon no one who was not a Muslim would be wanted to
teach Islamic studies. The politics of identity so clearly on display
in Jewish studies, for him, risked becoming the status quo in the
scholarly study of Islam (and for that matter of Buddhism, Hinduism, Christianity, and so on). That is, my friend implied that Islamic
studies as a discipline would soon purge itself of non-Muslims in the
same manner that Jewish studies is today largely bereft of non-Jews.
(The great paradox, however, is that the majority of students taking
Jewish studies courses in American universities—at least beyond the
East Coast corridor—are non-Jews.)

   And then there is Israel. What is the nature of the relationship
of Jewish studies to the State of Israel? Is it the goal of the scholar of Judaism in America to identify with it and to defend it at all
costs, even if one has real problems with the political actions that its
right-wing politicians take? I recall once giving a lecture at an area
synagogue about the "Arab Spring" and the Muslim Brotherhood,
wherein I argued that perhaps one of the places in the Middle East
where democracy was most under threat was in Israel on account
of the illiberal attitudes of many in the Haredi or ultra-Orthodox
community and the government. An audience member got up and
berated me, saying that, although I may be correct, he hoped that I
was not lecturing about such matters in my classes at the university
because it had the potential to make Jews and Israel look bad in the
eyes of non-Jews!

   This Israel-good/Arabs-bad binary—including its alternative,
the Israel-bad/Arabs-good binary—is an unfortunate reality on many
North American campuses. And unfortunately the scholar of Judaism
(not unlike the scholar of Islam) can find him- or herself caught in
the middle of such ideological battles. Is it part of this individual's
job description to offer him- or herself as the de facto defender of
Zionist causes and protector of Jewish students on campus?[1] Certainly the community and administrative expectations differ depending upon the campus in question. Large programs or departments
such as NYU's Skirball Department of Hebrew and Judaic Studies

or Stanford's Taube Center certainly allow for a greater amount of diversity on such matters than in those places where there is only one Jewish studies faculty member in largely Christocentric religious studies departments in, say, the Midwest. However, because roughly 95 percent of scholars of Judaism are ethnically and religiously Jewish, it is perhaps inevitable that they become metonymically identified, whether willingly or not, with either or both Israel and something that is frequently referred to as "the Jewish people."

There exist, in other words, real minefields in how Judaism is situated in the current moment. What I, an insider to the field, think Jewish studies is in my own mind and what someone like Russell McCutcheon, an outsider, considers it to be based on his own experiences is certainly not easily reconcilable. For me, at least on good days, Jewish studies represents the interdisciplinary study of Jewish peoples across time and geography. For him, including many of my other friends and colleagues from the more theoretically sophisticated North American Association for the Study of Religion (NAASR), Jewish studies represents all that is wrong with the academic study of religion: too introspective, too ethnic, too navel-gazing, and too willing to reify or essentialize data that it not unproblematically constructs as "Jewish."

The present volume is an attempt to reflect on these tensions,[2] if for no other reason than to clarify or at least taxonomize them in my own mind and for those experiencing a similar dissonance. It is perhaps worthwhile, I believe, to step back and ask such basic questions as, What is Jewish studies? How does it relate to the academic study of religion? My goal in asking these and related questions is twofold. First, to convince my colleagues working in theory and method in religious studies that Jewish data, and its theorizing, should be considered an important part of their conversations. Second, to try to convince my colleagues in Jewish studies that *some* of the theoretical and methodological concerns of religious studies can be useful in making Jewish studies, well, a tad less "ethnic."

Let me take a few paragraphs to clarify what I mean by religious studies. The history of the academic study of religion, as I have argued elsewhere (e.g., Hughes 2007, 2010a, 2012), is predicated on a set of largely Western and Christocentric categories that are subsequently retrofitted onto other cultures and earlier times with the express intent of carving out, examining, and describing a set of world "religions" (see further Fitzgerald 2000; Masuzawa 2005). Today, such categories are largely employed for the sake of articulating a set of vague similarities (e.g., prayer, belief, spirituality) between various religions with an eye toward some form of liberal Protestant ecumenicism. As others have well shown, this ecumenicism is often predicated on the claim that religious experience is somehow sui generis or unique and that differences between religions are based on the assumption that "the political," "the cultural," or "the ideological" impinges upon that which is perceived to be an almost ubiquitous access to the so-called "spiritual" (see, for example, McCutcheon 1997, 2005; Dubuisson 2003).

This assumption unfortunately discourages much interdisciplinary work. If religionists start from the assumption that religion is that which informs all other aspects of human creativity, there becomes no good reason to examine this creativity from other disciplinary perspectives. (As an aside, I once had a colleague who told me in all seriousness that she told her students that religious studies was the one *truly* interdisciplinary department!) This is ludicrous. An anthropologist would rightly proclaim that religionists ignore culture and the way "religion" (if they would even call it by this name) is lived and contested "on the ground." A political scientist would likewise ask quizzically about why religion cannot be reduced to the political or the ideological. The issue is not that people say they are religious, such a specialist in politics might well argue, but the motivating political and ideological forces that lead them to proclaim such utterances in the first place.

Such claims, it seems to me, largely derive from the desire on the part of religionists to make their field relevant at a time of increasing financial and administrative pressures within the contemporary university. They most likely arise genealogically from a distorted understanding of the work of Max Weber. It was his analysis of rational bourgeois capitalism, after all, that led him to survey the world's religions in search of the connection between economic formations and religious motivation. But, as far as I can tell, Weber never made the leap from his very specific analysis of the relationship between religion and economics to the sui generis and nonreductive claims that are some of the major hallmarks of the academic study of religion today. It is surely also related to the phenomenological claims of Mircea Eliade, probably one of the greatest popularizers of the academic study of religion in America. He argued that all religions shared a common sense of the sacred that had numerous manifestations in the various religions of the globe (see, e.g., Eliade 1958). Different cultures, then, were able to access the same sacred experience but did so through an intricate network of related morphological symbols.

This speculation about religion is perhaps best on display in a recent popular book by Stephen Prothero entitled *God Is Not One:*

The Eight Rival Religions That Run the World—and Why Their Differences Matter (2010). It is important not to assume—as Prothero does, as indeed so many in the discipline do—that a specific religion is tantamount to a culture's, for lack of a better term, *épistémè*. In other words, we cannot assume that if we read thirty-five pages on Judaism or Confucianism and then find ourselves at a later date in Jerusalem or Shanghai we will somehow become magically equipped to understand our foreign surroundings. Religion does not tell us about or help us understand culture (although interestingly understanding culture does provide us with the tools to understand "religion"). In like manner, religion does not tell us about or help us understand local political issues (again, though, the political and the ideological frequently give us insight into the so-called "religious").

So what does religion tell us about? The study of religion is, I maintain, an exercise in falsity. It means extracting one cultural or social formation from an intricate and conjoined matrix and then labeling it "religion." This "religion" is subsequently held up as the essence of the people from whom it was extracted. We should also keep in mind that most languages do not even have the word for religion and that this further adds to the falsity of the endeavor.

Religious studies, from this brief synopsis, is not necessarily a discipline in the best of academic health. However, it is one of the primary disciplinary units wherein Jewish data is analyzed, discussed, and taught. Like Jewish studies, moreover, it is an enterprise fraught with unchecked assumptions, with the reification of its main subject matter, and with the larger claim that its data is somehow special. One would think, then, that the academic study of Judaism could only be as good as the disciplinary home in which it was brought up. However, Jewish studies, as we shall see, has a history and a genealogy quite separate from religious studies, and only since about the 1970s have the two gravitated toward one another. Before this time, Jewish data tended to be studied and analyzed within Semitics departments, where it was often referred to as "Jewish Semitics." In keeping with the disciplinary focus of such departments, data deemed important was always premodern, textual, and almost universally written by males. However, since that time Jewish studies—at least as taught within departments of religious studies, which is my primary concern in the pages that follow—has developed some of the bad habits of the latter and, of course, vice versa. Yet, these bad habits are not solely the fault of the "parent" discipline of religious studies. The 1970s also witnessed an increased Jewish pride in the aftermath of the recapture of Jerusalem in the Six Day War, and also coincided with the rise of a host of ethnic or area studies to celebrate the traditionally excluded (e.g., black studies, women's studies).

The study that follows is an attempt to tell the story of the academic study of Judaism from the less traditional disciplinary perspective of religious studies, especially those discourses in the latter field that seek to interrogate and problematize the intellectual status quo. I say "less traditional" because this story is more customarily told using the narrative provided by history (see, for example, the excellent historiographical studies in Myers 1995, Wiese 2005, Brenner 2010). My goal in examining something similar, but using a religious studies "framework" is to try to provide a different type of narrative and one that, in so doing, seeks to mine the nature of the relationship between the academic study of religion and that of Judaism. This relationship, I submit, is one that is often assumed, but rarely analyzed in detail. It is, thus, necessary to try to understand the various ways in which Jewish studies constructs, discovers, and subsequently interprets its data. Why, for example, is Jewish data—or perhaps, more accurately, data that is constructed as "Jewish"—primarily studied within departments of religious studies? How, why, and when did these two "disciplines" come together? Do they inhibit or cross-pollinate one another?

To this end, what follows seeks to provide a quasigenealogical study, demonstrating where the academic study of Judaism began and why, tracing its development from Europe in the nineteenth century to America in the twentieth, and framing some of the challenges for the twenty first. I try to do this by focusing on a set of select case studies that provide what I consider to be windows onto a number of key issues in the scholarly—as opposed to religious—construction of Judaism. My concern is to try to provide answers to a series of questions: How did the academic study of Judaism migrate from Wissenschaft des Judentums (the science of Judaism) to Oriental studies, to what is today known as Jewish studies? What has religious studies done, and not done, for the academic study of Judaism? Why does Jewish studies always seem to fit so tenuously and ambiguously within religious studies? Has the latter discipline opened it up to new methods, or has it further contributed to its various assumptions and tendency to examine Jewish data in ways that refuse to connect them to larger cultural, social, and religious contexts?

My goal in providing a framework for these and related questions is to offer an extended essay on religious studies as much as on Jewish studies. If Jewish studies were unique or its set and range of issues of little concern to others, the present study would be largely irrelevant. However, the issues examined below—how data is imagined and constructed, the role of the insider/outsider, the tensions between scholar and community, and, finally, the rise of large foundations that sponsor research—are relevant to all those working in the human sciences.

No dataset, in other words, is inherently interesting. On the contrary, it becomes so only when it illumines a larger problem or more universal set of issues. In this respect, the story of the academic study of Judaism reveals some of the issues and problems of what happens when ethnicity and the politics of identity (disciplinary, religious, ethnic, or otherwise) meet scholarship. For the ways in which Judaism has been and continues to be situated has potential repercussions on the ways in which any religion—or any dataset, for that matter—is both perceived and/or situated. When scholarship confronts ethnicity, or when area studies becomes too introspective, the lines between scholarship and apologetics, academy and community, begin to blur.

Why Do Only Jews Study Jewish Studies?

Although I can provide no statistics, and my numbers are derived solely through unscientific perusals of Jewish studies offerings throughout the country and attendance at the Annual Meeting of the AJS, it is probably safe to say that well over 95 percent of those who teach Jewish studies are ethnically Jewish.[3] This is a huge number and, I would argue, is unparalleled in other fields and areas within the larger discipline of religious studies. I doubt, however, that such numbers are aberrant for other ethnic or area studies. This issue, however, might well be crucial to understanding Jewish studies as an academic field: Do those who study Jewish data perceive themselves to be working in area studies, religious studies, or some other discipline? How one answers this question will certainly have significant repercussions on the field.

The majority of scholars who study Buddhism or Islam, for example, are neither Buddhist nor Muslim. Although it certainly might be worth pointing out that many who do teach Buddhism (or Islam or any other religion) may well be converts to Buddhism (or Islam or the religion in question)—hence my friend's concerns about the future of Islamic studies. However, it is worth noting in this context that such individuals have probably converted to the religion in question only *after* they began to study it professionally. Whether because of some transference based on feelings that one has to become what one studies or because of some perceived lack in their own spiritual development, such individuals desire to identify spiritually or religiously with their object of study.

This is not true, for the most part, of Jewish studies. The overwhelming majority of scholars of Judaism identify religiously and/or ethnically as Jewish. Is no one else interested in studying Jewish data (with the obvious exception being the Hebrew Bible or Old Testament)? Why is it okay for a non-Hindu or a non-Muslim to study the religions of South Asia or the Middle East, but not for a non-Jew to study Judaism? Or, framed somewhat differently, is it non-Jews who do not want to study Judaism, or Jews who do not want non-Jews to study Judaism?

These are certainly different and difficult questions to answer. Why would non-Jews not want to study Judaism? Surely the old supersessionist argument (though certainly alive in certain quarters) that Judaism is a religion of the letter of the law does not hold much weight in the contemporary academy. Or perhaps Judaism is not exotic enough? Now recognized as one of the entrenched (if minuscule) religious traditions in America, Judaism might be regarded as much a part of the status quo as Christianity is. Or maybe it is the ethnic component of Jewish studies that makes non-Jews unwilling to study Judaism professionally—the fear that one may never break into the "inner sanctum" of the field owing to one's inherent marginal status?

But more problematic, what if Jewish studies defines its own ethnic borders? In which case, what if non-Jews who want to study Judaism are discouraged from doing so and then channeled into studying other religions? This identity politics might be, in part, explicable given that historically non-Jews have not necessarily been the most sensitive interpreters of the tradition, preferring instead to claim that Judaism is a tradition that has fulfilled its usefulness and been superseded by another religion (e.g., Christianity and Islam). This is certainly not to make the claim that the only way that one can study a religion is "sensitively"; but it is to argue that Judaism as a category or a trope in much non-Jewish theological writings of the past two millennia has been anything but disinterested (see, e.g., Hughes 2010b).

Related to this notion of defining disciplinary borders is the fact that the academic study of Judaism took a strong turn inward in the late 1960s. This was, as mentioned above, the time of the 1967 war and the recovery of Jerusalem. All things Arab became bad, and Jewish data could now be studied using a set of internal criteria. This becomes problematic when it is remembered that many Jews, for much of history, lived in Arabic cultures and articulated Judaism using the theological categories of Islam. Reliance on other traditions or even other theoretical frameworks became increasingly problematic because they threatened or impeded the self-perceived uniqueness of Jewish data. This newly found sense of pride translated into the notion that the academic study of Judaism was no longer as interested in the theoretical and methodological apparatuses of other disciplines, something that it had been since the origins of Jewish studies in Germany in the nineteenth century.

The "Jewish Studies" of the Present Study

Jewish studies is a very diverse field, one with a lengthy and very impressive history. Some of the towering names of twentieth century scholarship—Harry A. Wolfson (1887–1974), Gershom Scholem (1897–1982), and Salo W. Baron (1895–1989)—engaged in pioneering research on Judaism, showing how it was in conversation with the larger intellectual and cultural milieux in which Jews lived. These individuals, with the exception of Wolfson (who was trained at Harvard), received their doctoral training in Europe, and they all had radically different ideas about the nature and contours of what Judaism was and how it should be studied (see, for example, Jonathan Cohen 2007, 1–6). To make the claim, then, that there exists one way to study or analyze "Judaism," as the careers of these three individuals clearly reveal, is both to oversimplify and to make a set of categorical assumptions that are unsupportable. My goal, to reiterate, is not to reduce this complexity to a set of axiomatic claims, but to try to classify the study of Judaism.

Baron, the Nathan L. Miller Professor of Jewish History, Literature, and Institutions at Columbia University, for example, was one of the earliest scholars to hold an endowed chair in Jewish studies at a university. Whereas prior to him Jewish topics in America tended to be studied primarily in departments of Semitics, wherein the primary interest was in things ancient, Baron insisted upon being hired in the history department at Columbia (Liberles 1997, 2–3). Equally at home in things ancient, medieval, and modern, Baron did much to establish Jewish studies as an academic discipline in the United States. Reacting against the "lachrymose" approach of an earlier generation of primarily European-Jewish scholars—most notably Heinrich Graetz (see chapter 2 in this book)—Baron sought to focus on the dynamic and life-affirming nature of Jewish history. In his eighteen-volume magnum opus, *The Social and Religious History of the Jews* (1952–1983),

Baron integrated what he considered to be the religious aspect of Jewish history into the larger dimension of Jewish life and, in so doing, tried to fit the history of Jews into the broader study of the eras and societies in which they lived.

Just a few years prior to Baron's appointment as the Nathan L. Miller Professor, Harry Austryn Wolfson was appointed professor of Hebrew literature and philosophy at Harvard in 1925. Like Baron, Wolfson was interested in showing the correspondence between Judaism and the broader cultural and intellectual contexts in which Jews lived. Unlike the historian Baron, however, the philosopher Wolfson located the most dynamic features of this correspondence in the medieval philosophical tradition. Writing in the *Menorah Journal* in 1921, prior to his appointment to the Harvard faculty, Wolfson remarks,

> For I believe, just as our pious ancestors believed, though for different reasons, that the Talmud with its literature is the most promising field of study, the most fertile field of original research and investigation. But I believe that medieval Jewish philosophy is the only branch of Jewish literature, next to the Bible, which binds us to the rest of the literary world. In it we meet on common ground with civilized Europe and with part of civilized Asia and civilized Africa. Medieval philosophy is one philosophy written in three languages, Arabic, Hebrew, and Latin, and among these Hebrew holds the central and most important position. In it we have the full efflorescence of Arabic thought and the bud of much of scholasticism. (Wolfson 1921, 32–33)

This passage is remarkable for numerous reasons. In it, Wolfson articulates a tension that has reverberated and will continue to do so through the length and breadth of Jewish studies. Although there is a tendency, let us call it "particularistic," to study traditional texts such as the Talmud and other works of rabbinic literature as the unique products of an insular Jewish tradition in dialogue with itself,[4] there exits a competing tendency, the "universalist," that looks to philosophical texts to see the cross-pollination of Jewish and other cultures.[5] Whereas Wolfson here argues that the former may well prove to be the most interesting for showing the originality of Jews and Judaism, it is the latter that makes Jews "European" and an intimate part of Western civilization (J. Cohen 1997, 59–63).

The tension between showing Jews to be part of and "influenced" by the larger cultures in which they dwelt and the impulse to make Jews sui generis is one that, as we shall see in the pages that follow, runs throughout much of the scholarship on Jews and Judaism. It is a tension, moreover, with a religious resonance, one that returns us to the biblical notion of Jewish chosenness. What "chosenness" means is a question that has preoccupied theologians and philosophers since the closing of the biblical canon. Despite the secular or quasi-secular nature of Jewish studies, this theme of chosenness nevertheless remains. Are Jews like other peoples or distinct from them? Does its diasporic character and Holocaust make Judaism unique or do the manifold cultures produced by Jews reflect and draw on those produced by non-Jews, such that the borders between what is "Jewish" and what is "non-Jewish" blur and are only reified by later interpreters (including contemporary scholars)? How one ultimately answers such questions ultimately determines how one situates Judaism. Such answers, moreover, are not simply scholarly, but intimately connected to a host of other, nonscholarly issues.

Unlike Wolfson and Baron, Gershom Scholem—founder of the academic study of Jewish mysticism and professor at the Hebrew University of Jerusalem from 1933 until his retirement in 1965—argued that the genius of Judaism resided in the irrational. Dissatisfied with the liberal bourgeois Judaism of his own upbringing in Germany, something that he found reflected in the academic approach to Judaism in his own day, Scholem sought to break from both (Biale 1982, 1–8). In his opinion, it was the mythical and mystical components of the tradition that were as important as, if not more so, than the rational ones articulated by the likes of Wolfson and his German-Jewish predecessors. For Scholem, it was these components that represented the living core of Judaism. Yet, because they were irrational, they were to be studied on their own, untouched by the rational and rationalizing tendencies of Jewish universalism. Writing against the German historical and philological tradition, Scholem boldly proclaimed that

> New concepts and new categories, new institutions and new daring, are required here: a "critique of the critique," the dismantling of the dismantling, and the use without fear of both horns of historical criticism. From now on, the creative destruction of scientific criticism which examines hearts and innards via the documents of the past serves a different function: not the washing and embalming of the dead body, but the discovery of its hidden life by removing the masks and the curtain which had hidden it, and the

> misleading descriptions . . . [This will] serve as a produc-
> tive decoding of the secret writing of the past, of the great
> symbols of our life within history. (Scholem 1997, 67)

For Scholem here the historical and rational understanding of Judaism
is stultifying. He perceives the historian to stand over Judaism with
the cold disinterest of the pathologist. Although his remarks above,
as I shall argue in chapter 2, are somewhat unfair, Scholem contends
that the real life and genius pulsating throughout Judaism reside in
the mystical and potentially anarchic subterranean caverns of its messianic impulse (Scholem 1971b; see the comments in Dan 1994, 73–78).

The tension between the universalistic and particularistic interpretations of Judaism—itself reflecting the extrospective and introspective elements present in Jewish texts—is one that we shall witness
time and again in the chapters that follow. Certainly in this regard
Jewish studies is not unlike other area studies or even other religious
traditions that Judaism often finds itself cohabiting with in departments of religious studies. What perhaps sets Jewish studies apart
from the scholarly study of other religious traditions, however, is
that the overwhelming majority of those who engage in Jewish studies religiously and ethnically identify with their object of study. And
although they may take highly critical approaches to their various
datasets, scholars of Judaism, more than scholars of any other tradition, are—correctly or incorrectly is not the issue here—seen as engaging in apologetics. This returns us to Russell McCutcheon's remarks
with which I opened this introduction. For him, like many others
interested in theoretical and critical questions, Jewish studies represents the classic paradigm of "special pleading."

I engaged in this brief survey of Baron, Wolfson, and Scholem
in order to show the complexity of my dataset. A simple reading
of these three individuals—taken for the moment as metonyms for
the entire field of Jewish studies—militates against tidy or monolithic
assumptions about what Jewish studies has been, is, or should be. It is,
in other words, not easy to synthesize into a coherent narrative how
Judaism has been studied in the course of the nineteenth and twentieth centuries—centuries that have been marked by mass migrations,
fights for political emancipation, anti-Semitism, Zionism and its quest
to find a solution to the "Jewish question," the destruction of six mil-
lion Jews and a way of life in Europe, and finally the nationalist pride
that coincides with the formation and the subsequent military might
of the State of Israel. This historical backdrop makes it impossible
simply to write these scholars off as apologists or Jewish studies off

as an apologetical discipline. Certainly all the scholars to be surveyed below had distinct ideas about what the essence of Judaism was and how Judaism fitted within broader cultural contexts. And even though essentialism today is, for the most part, out of fashion, we cannot simply dismiss a scholar such as Scholem—one of the luminaries of the twentieth century by any standards—as an essentialist who was apologizing for Jews and Judaism.

Breakdown of Chapters

The following chapter ("Authenticity, Identity, Scholarship") begins with a controversy that erupted at Queens College in New York City when a non-Jew, Thomas Bird, was appointed to be the director of the interdisciplinary Jewish studies program. It uses this controversy as a segue to reflect upon notions of Jewish (and non-Jewish) identity and its role in the academic study of Judaism. The chapter then switches focus and begins to explore the trope of "the Jew" among some of the early theoreticians either influential in religious studies (e.g., Karl Marx) or housed within departments of religious studies (e.g., Mircea Eliade). Such theorists have used the so-called Jewish question as a way to articulate their respective intellectual agendas, many of which are based on traditional anti-Semitic stereotypes. The tension between the supersessionist and the anti-Semitic on the one hand, and the identity politics of the contemporary moment, on the other are, I wish to suggest, certainly and intimately related to one another.

Following this, chapter 2 ("Encountering Tradition: The Search for a Jewish Essence") begins at the beginning, as it were, examining some of the material and intellectual contexts behind the rise of Wissenschaft des Judentums (science of Judaism) in Germany in the nineteenth century. My goal in this chapter is not original but synthetic as I try to demonstrate some of the ideological and political concerns behind the rise of the academic study of Judaism. From its origins in the nineteenth century, the academic study of Judaism has largely been bound up with the apologetical desire to show that Jews and Judaism were normal. Yet, as some Jewish intellectuals sought to situate Judaism in history, others (e.g., Hermann Cohen, Franz Rosenzweig) sought to locate it outside of history. This struggle for the essence of Judaism has played an important role, I suggest, in the study of Judaism ever since.

Chapter 3 ("Imagining Judaism: Scholar, Community, Identity") focuses on the migration of Jewish studies out of Germany, to Israel and to the United States, at the beginning of the twentieth century. At this point, Jewish studies did not so much lose its earlier ideological focus, but developed new ones in response to the changing circumstances of Jews in each place. In Israel, for example, the study of Judaism—now done in Hebrew as opposed to German—became part and parcel of the Zionist desire to create and establish a new national homeland for Jews. In America, by contrast, Jews sought the inclusion of Jewish topics in American universities and did their best to fund privately positions therein. The result was that the scholar of Judaism became a symbol for the desires and hopes of the larger Jewish community.

Chapter 4 ("Take Ancient Judaism for Example: Five Case Studies") uses case studies to examine some of the ways that scholars in the middle of the twentieth century configured the study of Jewish data with larger trends in religious studies. Three of these scholars are Jewish (Morris Jastrow, Jacob Neusner, J. Z. Smith), and two are non-Jews (George Foot Moore, Erwin Goodenough). This religioethnic difference, however, does *not* lead into tidy bifurcations, as we might be accustomed to believe, wherein the latter tend to be more critical than the former. On the contrary, ethnic background played little role in determining how each one of these individuals either conceived of or taxonomized Judaism. The thread that unites them is that all work on premodern forms of Judaism, choosing to focus their attention on either biblical or postbiblical (i.e., rabbinic) forms.

Chapter 5 ("Private Foundations Encounter Judaism") explores one of the most important issues facing the academic study of Judaism at the present moment: the rise of private foundations that seek inroads into the academy—and presumably the intellectual legitimation that this provides—by funding various programs, professorships, and conferences in both Jewish studies and Israel studies at North American and Israeli universities. These foundations, in their various ways, seek to transform the academic study of Judaism, and they desire to do so based on their own ideological agendas. The unfortunate result is that Jewish studies, rather than liberating itself from its ideological heritage, actually risks re-embracing it. Certainly hiring in Jewish studies in this country has always involved the financial support of individual donors, but foundations do not simply want to support Jewish studies or Israel studies; they want to transform them and change them from within based on their own understanding of what Judaism is.

The final chapter ("Future Prospects") switches focus and attempts to offer, based on the previous chapters, an analysis of the future of Jewish studies. How might the academic study of Judaism learn from its past? In this regard it follows the more general trajectories in the humanities that seek to query and interrogate identity and identity formations.

Conclusions

I began this introduction focusing on the comments of those like Russell McCutcheon and others associated with critical discourses in religious studies who want to see in Jewish studies the quintessence of special pleading and the end product of what happens when the study of religion is carried out solely by "insiders." There is certainly some truth to these assumptions. For Jewish studies, like any area studies program that came into its own in the 1960s and 1970s, attempts to account for that which the traditional and mainstream departments and disciplines had ignored. However, in doing this it has paradoxically reified Jewish data and something vaguely referred to as "*the* Jewish experience."

However, there is a danger in simply writing Jewish studies off as an ethnic enclave existing within larger and more pluralistic departments of religious studies. In so doing, for example, we ignore the larger intellectual context in which Jewish studies originated and developed over the last two hundred years, including its response to—among other things—anti-Semitism and the Holocaust. In looking at the origins, rise, and development of Jewish studies, we are also able to learn something about the larger discipline of religious studies: its own set of assumptions and how it, in turn, privileges and marginalizes data. The story of Jewish studies is not something of interest only to those who study Judaism; it should be compelling reading to anyone interested in the formation of disciplines.

1

Authenticity, Identity, Scholarship

In 1996 there erupted a controversy at Queens College in the City University of New York (CUNY). The dean of the college had just appointed Thomas Bird, a Russian and Yiddish literature professor, as the head of the interdisciplinary Jewish studies program. Although Bird was a scholar of Yiddish language and culture, and a longtime activist on behalf of Soviet Jews, he was not Jewish. Samuel Heilman, Bird's colleague and an Orthodox Jew, objected to his appointment. He reasoned that because Bird was not Jewish, did not know Hebrew (even though he knew Yiddish), and had not published articles in mainstream Jewish studies journals, he was unqualified to direct the Jewish studies program (Greenberg 1996). Little over two weeks into his new and now highly contentious position, Bird resigned, citing what he called "primitive religious bigotry." He claimed that "it is impossible not to conclude that the attempt to trash my academic record and standing in the community through insinuation and omission is anything other than a fig leaf for objections to my being a gentile" (Greenberg 1996).

At the height of the controversy, just after Bird had resigned his position, Heilman, the principle accuser, published a short essay entitled "Who Should Direct Jewish Studies at the University?" Therein he mentioned that he was less interested in whether or not Bird was Jewish than the fact that he did not have a PhD (although an associate professor, he was still a doctoral candidate at Princeton). In particular, Heilman writes,

> If the university singles out Jewish Studies and appoints a person to head it who does not come from that ethnic group, at a time when all its other ethnic studies programs are headed by members of those ethnic groups, who does not have the same high academic qualifications as those in other programs, and when the administration chooses

17

> not to appoint as Jewish Studies director one of the many
> professors on campus who hold the highest academic
> degrees and have distinguished reputations and records
> in Jewish Studies, and read and understand Hebrew in
> favor of someone who does not, then there ought to be
> some compelling reason for that decision. (Heilman 1996)

This is a strange claim. Since other area studies at his university happen to have directors or chairs that are the same ethnicity, gender, or color as the administrative unit they lead, Heilman thinks that Jewish studies should be no different. If others are engaged in identity politics, he reasons, so, too, must Jewish studies. Heilman also faults Bird for the fact that he does not know Hebrew and, in so doing, makes the problematic assertion that Hebrew somehow represents *the* authentic Jewish language. Bird's lack of knowledge in Hebrew—at least in Heilman's worldview—seems to disqualify him from administering a program in Jewish studies. This creates two problems. First, would Heilman have put up such linguistic objections if Bird was Jewish? That is, would Heilman object to a Jewish director of Jewish studies who did not know Hebrew? Second, and relatedly, Heilman ignores the fact that Jews throughout their long and diverse history have not only spoken but also articulated Judaism using Greek, Aramaic, Arabic, and countless European vernaculars. The result is that all these languages could just as easily be regarded as "Jewish" languages (Hughes 2012). Heilman, in other words, is making a number of normative judgments that should make us uncomfortable: not only does he attempt to articulate what is authentically "Jewish" and "not-Jewish," but he engages in a slippery argument that those most qualified to direct (and presumably teach) Jewish studies are Jews. He nowhere says, however, what kind of Jews. Are Reform Jews better than secular ones? Does this, then, make Conservative Jews better than Reform? Or, are Orthodox (or, even, ultra-Orthodox) the most qualified because they are somehow deemed the most "authentic"?

Although in principle he states that his objection is with Bird's academic credentials, it soon becomes evident that this is not all that Heilman has in mind. For, in addition to the above statement, he claims that Jewish studies faculty "can and do also serve as role models for students and the larger Jewish community, embodying what it means to take Jewish life and culture seriously." Presumably by this latter comment—that a director of Jewish studies needs to "take Jewish life and culture seriously"—Heilman means that one can only do this by being Jewish and that a non-Jew cannot presumably undertake such activity or at least do so with any degree of competence. Again, this creates a host of uncomfortable distinctions: does a Jew who is *shomer shabbas* (i.e., follow all the legal restrictions of the Sabbath), for example, take Judaism more "seriously" than a Jew who does not? The repercussions of such statements are problematic on a number of levels.

Whether he knows it or not, Heilman, trained as a sociologist, invokes a well-worn trope in religious studies, that of taking Judaism (or, religion in general) "seriously." This trope—and all of the unchecked assumptions that it implies—forms the subject matter of this chapter. What Heilman clearly verbalizes, a position that I have heard articulated in numerous other settings, is that non-Jews should not or cannot study Jews or Judaism. (Although, to be fair, I have also heard the opposite claim, namely, that what Jewish studies truly needs is for more non-Jews to study Judaism.) Whether because they lack the specialized linguistic training, as Heilman implies, or because they do not know what it means to live or experience the world "Jewishly," the role of the non-Jew in the academic study of Judaism potentially raises a host of problems. Just as the "Jew" has functioned as the symbol par excellence against which Christian Europe has largely defined itself since the time of Jesus, the "non-Jew" now becomes a symbol whereby Jewish studies articulates itself, its object of study, and attempts to define who possesses the authority to study it properly.

The Heilman-Bird controversy provides an interesting, if acute, example of the way in which identity, authenticity, and scholarship play out in the academic study of Judaism. In so doing, it also functions metonymically for a set of issues that plagues and ultimately threatens the well being of the larger field of religious studies. That is, how does scholarship—whether associated with Judaism or with any other religion—create or establish a set of conditions that manufacture, assert, and subsequently disseminate notions of identity and authenticity? Since the academic study of religion purports, according to some, to study that which is most dear and precious to people (i.e., their "inner" and "spiritual" lives), there exists the dangerous assumption that only those who have had the same kind of "inner experiences" are uniquely qualified to study and write about the religion in question.

Such an assumption, however, is predicated on a number of nebulous concepts that are impossible to verify or subject to any sort of intellectual scrutiny. What, for example, is an "inner experience" (see the discussion in Scharf 1999)? Even if we could ascertain what it is, who would be in a position to adjudicate what counts as an authentic "inner experience" and what counts as an inauthentic one? The answer to questions such as these is political and ideological, not natural or scientific. Such "experiences," moreover, are often assumed to be irreducible as opposed to culturally or ideologically constructed. This means that religion in general—or religions (e.g., Judaism) in particular—is assumed to possess an essence that cannot be reduced to other material or historical forces (for a critique of this, see McCutcheon 1997, 35–37). As others have well shown, however, the discourse of an irreducible or sui generis experience or set of experiences is of fairly recent provenance, largely operating as a rhetorical response to certain critiques of religion in the West, most notably Kant's reduction of religion to a set of ethical claims (see, e.g., Proudfoot 1985; Scharf 1999). Despite this, many—both inside and outside of the academy—have no qualms about taking this manufactured and ideologically charged concept of experience and then claiming that it exists naturally in the world. These "experiences"—in turn connected to an "essence"—are subsequently reified as "Jewish" (or "Muslim," or "Buddhist," or whatever other religion one happens to study) and then projected onto distant times and places.

This projection, however, is tied to both essentialism and identity politics. How can we assume, for example, that the way in which Judaism was constructed in third-century CE Palestine (or eleventh-century Cordoba) is the same as that constructed in contemporary America? Not only is third-century Palestinian Judaism pretalmudic,[1] but the varieties of Judaism in contemporary America did not even exist in the third or eleventh century. Despite its constructed nature, we frequently feel comfortable speaking about "*the* Jewish experience"—not even the less, but still problematic, "Jewish experiences"— as if it (a) really existed and (b) it is monolithic at all times and all places. Yet, as Russell McCutcheon has well argued, the attempt to create an irreducible religious experience—or one of its numerous species, such as "Jewish experience"—is primarily a sociopolitical claim (McCutcheon 1997, 16). This claim not only reifies a particular "experience"; it also authorizes—as we see in the Heilman-Bird controversy—those who can (or cannot) study it.

The academic study of Judaism, as we shall see in the following chapter, was largely created for apologetical purposes, namely, to show non-Jews that Jews, too, possessed an essence that manifested itself in the historical record. Jewish history could, in turn, be quantified and taxonomized in the same manner that the histories of other peoples/nations could. Because of this, and owing to the fact that Jewish topics were forbidden from being taught in German universities and were instead largely taught at denominationally affiliated seminaries, non-Jews tended not to be interested in studying Judaism or Jewish data.[2] Now, however, as Jewish studies has become a valid field of study that has become firmly entrenched within the humanities and social sciences curriculum, Judaism ought to be the subject of analysis in the same manner that every other religion is; that is, something that can be studied by those who are of the particular religion and those who are not. Yet, despite the change in intellectual contexts and the inclusion and normalization of Jewish studies within the contemporary university, the tension nevertheless remains concerning who is authorized to study Jews and Judaism.

David Gelernter's Judaism: A Way of Being

A good example of the reification and essentialization of Judaism to make it conform to a prefabricated set of expectations is David Gelernter's *Judaism: A Way of Being* (2009). Gelernter, a professor of computer science at Yale University, received permanent damage to his right hand and eye on account of a mail bomb sent to him by Theodore Kaczynski (the "Unabomber"). Prior to the bombing, Gelernter identified as a secular Jew, afterward becoming increasingly religious.[3] Gelernter is also a frequent columnist for neo-conservative magazines such as *Commentary* and the *Weekly Standard*. This political position seems, as we shall see shortly, to have made its way into his *Judaism: A Way of Being*. This latter work—bankrolled by Roger Hertog, the conservative American philanthropist and chairman of the Tikvah Fund (see chapter 5 in this work)[4]—basically amounts to neoconservative screed for a particular version of Judaism, that is, Orthodoxy, that the author deems most authentic (for a critique of the Tikvah fund more generally and its desire to situate itself within academic study of Judaism, see Braiterman 2011).

Although he has no academic training in either religious studies or Jewish studies, Gelernter takes it upon himself in *Judaism: A Way of Being* to encapsulate the religion for what he considers to be a lost generation. It is, in other words, a fairly typical book written by a Jew for other Jews warning them about the evils of secularism and intermarriage. The difference, however, and what makes it interesting in the present context, is that it just happens to be published by Yale University Press. In the book's opening, Gelernter argues that "unless the *essence* of Judaism is written down plainly as can be, the loosening grip most American Jews maintain on the religion of their ancestors will fail completely, and the community will plummet into the anonymous depths of history" (2009, 3; my italics). What might this essence consist of? For Gelernter, it coincides, as he makes clear on the book's first page, with normative, that is "Orthodox" Judaism (2009, ix). Orthodox Judaism's teachings about Jewish chosenness, gender relations, and the answers it supplies to "the great questions of human existence" are the only ones that the author finds worthy of consideration (for a critical and informed review, see the comments in E. Wolfson 2010). Orthodoxy, for the author, represents "Judaism at full strength, straight up; no water, no soda, aged in oak for three thousand years" (2009, xi). Rival Judaisms—Reform, Conservative, egalitarian, secular, and the like—are, in comparison, implied to be watered down.

Not only has Gelernter defined Judaism's essence as that which corresponds to Orthodoxy, not surprisingly his own denominational commitment, but he goes on to project its essence into the spiritual core of Western civilization. In an appendix entitled "What Makes Judaism the Most Important Intellectual Development in Western History?" he writes that Judaism

> [h]as given moral and spiritual direction to Jewish, Christian, and Muslim society, and indirectly to the modern and postmodern worlds. But not only that. Judaism formed our idea of God and man, of sanctity, justice, and love: love of God, family, nation, and mankind. But not only that. Judaism created the ideal of congregational worship that made the church and the mosque possible. But not only that. Much of the modern liberal state grew out of Judaism by way of American Puritans, neo-Puritans, and quasi-Puritans who revered the Hebrew Bible and pondered it constantly. (2009, 198)

This essence of Judaism, moving effortlessly throughout human history, is the origin of virtually everything that we are supposed to hold dear in the modern world. No mention is made that such ideas took shape through a synergy of "Jewish" and "non-Jewish" ideas—indeed to such an extent that it is probably impossible to pull them apart and decipher which is which. Many of the pieties and platitudes that we find in works such as Gelernter's are more appropriate for the synagogue than the academy. For it is ultimately in the former that matters such as identity creation and maintenance are never questioned, but assumed as given, something handed down from generation to generation.

Identity politics with a chaser of neo-conservativism (to keep Gelernter's alcoholic metaphor) will only end badly for Jewish studies. Once one claims to know the essence of a tradition, what it is and what it is not, inquiry gives way to apologetics, and scholarship gives way to ideology.[5] Gelernter's work is not a disinterested or objective work of scholarship, even though the Yale University Press imprimatur may make it appear otherwise. Rather, it is a highly partisan account of Judaism based on and funded by very interested constituents outside of the academy. Perhaps if a Jewish theological press had published it, I might not take it to task in the manner that I have here. However, the fact that it is written by a nonexpert and financed by a neoconservative philanthropist seeking to make inroads for right wing causes in Israel and in Jewish studies in America potentially sets a very dangerous precedent.

Although Gelernter's argument is different from the likes of Heilman, it nonetheless emerges from the same privileged sphere. There is an essence to Judaism that only Jews are able to access owing to their birthright or commitment to a particular denomination. Those outside the privileged sphere—non-Jews, non-Orthodox—have no or little existential access to it. This, I submit, is all that is wrong with Jewish studies at this particular moment. And unless Jewish studies confronts this, it risks being relegated to the back room of area studies and becoming confined to the dark domain of identity politics.

Dislocating Judaism's Essence

Problems inevitably follow whenever one wants to limit who should be able to study religious data within an academic setting (with the obvious exception of academic qualification).[6] Heilman's desire to control who can or cannot administer Jewish studies and Gelernter's desire to proclaim that one particular version of Judaism, that is, his own, is normative reeks of apologetics. This need to find an essence that can somehow explain all later "manifestations" of the tradition is certainly not confined to the likes of Heilman's desire to maintain ethnic purity or Gelernter's misinformed apologetics for Orthodox Judaism. Many introductory textbooks also seek to discover Judaism's essence. In his *Introducing Judaism*, for example, Eliezer Segal defines this as the Law:

> It must be remembered that for Jews . . . the ultimate expression of divine revelation is in the form of laws. This is certainly true for traditional Jews who believe that the most momentous event in history was when God revealed the Torah to the children of Israel at Mount Sinai. The Torah

consists primarily of laws and commandments, and it has always been assumed that the intensive study of religious law is a fundamental act of religious devotion. Jewish religious law encompasses, not only matters of belief, liturgy, and ritual, but also covers the full range of civil and criminal laws. For Jews, all these laws have their origin in a divine revelation, and their observance forms the basis of the eternal covenant between God and the people of Israel. (2009, 57)

Here Segal, an Orthodox Jew, not surprisingly makes the law and its observance into the essence of Judaism. It is, according to him, a divine revelation that *all* Jews (no mention of which Jews in particular) believe is the sine qua non of the covenant between God and Israel. What do we do with all those Jews, perhaps even the majority of Jews, who do not believe this?

Equally problematic is the attempt to define ethics or ethical monotheism as the essence of Judaism. In an essay entitled "Singularity: The Universality of Jewish Particularism," Richard A. Cohen reflects upon the ethical mission of Judaism as witnessed in two important twentieth-century Jewish thinkers, Elijah Benamozegh and Emmanuel Levinas. Cohen writes of Judaism's "holy mission":

Judaism is a religion not merely of tolerance, if by tolerance one means that one grits ones teeth and provisionally endures alternatives. Rather, it is a religion of tolerance whose divinely revealed teachings of universal morality and justice aim to produce not a mirror image of itself, but a righteous humanity, whatever the denominational affiliation of that humanity. With the same breath with which Benamozegh and Levinas insist upon the fundamental and irreducible relevance of Judaism for Jews and non-Jews, they also insist, to the same Jews—without any diminution, condescension or duplicity—on the irreducible relevance, the universality, of Judaism for all humanity. To be chosen is to be responsible for each and everyone, Jew and non-Jew alike, "widow, orphan, and stranger." (Cohen 2010, 257–58)

Cohen here eloquently molds Judaism in the crucible provided by the ethical thought of Levinas, and the entire Jewish tradition is then retroactively interpreted in his light. This thought, revealed at Sinai and forming the essence of Judaism's universal ethical mission, is what defines Judaism, representing—in the words of Thomas Cahill—"the gift of the Jews" (1998).

The desire to uncover in Judaism an essence—be it the Law (à la Gelernter or Segal) or ethical monotheism (à la Cohen or Cahill)—has, for various reasons, configured with the notion that Jews themselves possess a unique essence that emerges from Judaism and that differentiates them from all other peoples.[7] This may be the modern iteration of the biblical notion of "chosenness," or it may simply be another example of a small minority stressing its particularism or ethnic pride. Whatever the reason, the repercussion seems to be similar: Jews possess an essence that somehow makes them predisposed or that puts them in a commanding position to study this essence, their very own essence, in history.

This tense intersection of ethnicity, identity, and scholarship represents one of the major issues currently facing the academic study of Judaism. Identity politics subscribes to a particular group a set of traits or characteristics that all members of a particular social category or group are believed to share. These traits or characteristics can subsequently be "located" or "found" in the historical record and in various times and places. Recent work by sociologists (e.g., Bourdieu 1984) and anthropologists (e.g., Bayart 2005), however, has stressed the cultural construction and manufacture of identity formations. Rather than assume that such identities are given in the natural world, then, we should perhaps focus on how they are actively constructed and imagined. In this respect, the work of Jonathan Boyarin is instructive. He writes in his "Responsive Thinking: Cultural Studies and Jewish Historiography" that much academic writing in Jewish studies is predicated on "our hold on some attachment to a positive projection of some *sui generis* core of group identity" (2008, 41). This sui generis core, predicated as it is upon boundary construction and maintenance, has largely dictated the way the field has thought of and constructed Jewishness in both the past and the present, deeming what counts as an authentic expression and what does not. But such decisions of authenticity or inauthenticity must be appreciated for what they are: choices based on ideology, not ontology. Boyarin concludes his essay with the claim that

> [r]ather than fix on a supposedly delimited time and space as the guarantor of the purest approach to truth, let us be aware that we are constantly tacking between two formations of identity, the one (the notion of "ourselves") inescapable for continued human life and being continually

reshaped and nurtured by the other (the "past" in its rel-
ics), and attend to our work as not simply the *knowing*, but
rather the active *making* or *performance* of history. Maybe
in that . . . , rather than be ultimately tempted to conclude
that the question of any profound commonalities among
Jews through time and space is a trick of the present, we
will allow ourselves to remain humbled—not hobbled—by
Paul Gilroy's reminder that "the fragile psychological, emotional, and cultural correspondence which connect diaspora
populations in spite of their manifest differences are often
apprehended only fleetingly and in ways that persistently
confound the protocols of academic orthodoxy." (Boyarin
2008, 43–44)

Boyarin's comments here are instructive for several reasons. For one
thing, the creation of identity—now as in the past—is the figment of
genealogical memory. In our quest for origins and authenticity, we
tend to reify the history of lineage found in so much of our sources,
and we do so, moreover, to such an extent that this lineage becomes
elided into our own being and fabric. In this regard, Jewish studies,
like any area studies, reaffirms the myth of ethnic continuity or purity
through the ages. Our challenge, as intimated in Boyarin's comments
above, is not to assume that the borderlines between Jew and non-Jew
represent real lines that exist naturally in the world, but to question
when and how they came about, to see what kind of taxonomic work
they provided in the past, including for whom and for what purposes.

Once we situate the various Judaisms of the past within the
shared cultural universes in which they were actively produced, we
hopefully begin to modify our understanding of what constitutes
"Judaism" and "non-Judaism." But until we do this, we will remain
beholden to the same form of identity politics that has generated—
and indeed continues to power—so much of the thinking within the
field. As long as we tend to believe that the distant past is, again in
the words of Boyarin, "somehow fixed and therefore better known
than our own messy present (Boyarin 2008, 42), we will continue to
reify something called "Jewishness" and continue to persevere in our
desire to perceive its most authentic iterations in the historical record.

There is no such thing as "true" Jewishness, just as there cannot be any such thing as "true" Muslimness, "true" Christianness, or
any other such entity. Jewishness, like any other identity formation,
is continually imagined (and reimagined), invented (and reinvented),
and produced (and reproduced). And if there is no such thing as

"true" Jewishness, its recuperation—whether simple or otherwise—becomes entirely problematic. On this subject of communal invention or reinvention, Miriam Bodian's study of the invention of Sephardic Jewishness among Jews after their departure from Spain in 1492 is telling. She writes,

> Living in Calvinist Amsterdam, they were more conspicu-ously Iberian than ever before. This was a source of pride and an important component of their developing sense of collective self. As practicing Jews in a Christian environ-ment, there was also a clear religious boundary separating them from the majority society. Both in the habits they had assimilated from Spanish and Portuguese society and in their practice of Jewish law, they suddenly became what they had never been before, a well-defined group. (Bodian 1999, 18)

To tell this story from the perspective of "Jewish pride," the way so many of the students I teach conceive of it, the Iberian Jews—perse-cuted and under pressure to convert in Spain—kept the spirit of Juda-ism alive in their hearts and homes (far from public gaze). And, once religiously free in a place like Amsterdam, they simply returned to their Jewish "heritage." But such a religiously inspired narrative—as Bodian's work so tellingly reminds us—ignores the task of communal invention and reinvention in the formation of collective identity.

The Insider/Outsider Problem

The central question in the academic study of religion is how to under-stand properly the various texts, actions, behaviors, rituals, and so on that practitioners describe as "religious." The professional religionist is presented with a great deal of religious "data" and must decide how to explain them, interpret them, and ultimately classify them. This gives way to a fairly vociferous debate known as the "insider/outsider problem."

An insider approach—alternatively called an emic approach—is one that tries to understand religion from the perspective of reli-gious practitioners. It involves looking at religious texts and religious rituals in order to find out the significance of these for practitioners and subsequently describes their contents and performances to oth-ers. Many who privilege the insider perspective believe that there is something unique about religion and religious experience that can never be reduced to something else (e.g., culture, society, politics) or explained away. The insider approach represents, in sum, the effort to understand religious thought and behavior primarily from the point of view of religious persons.

The outsider perspective—or alternatively, the etic approach—is one that refuses to explain religion using the categories and terms of reference that religious people use. As such, it attempts to import categories from the outside in an attempt to interpret or explain religious data. This can be reductionist; witness Sigmund Freud's desire to "reduce" religion to psychological function and explain it using the language of psychology or Emile Durkheim's reduction of religion to social processes. Increasingly, such approaches tend to question the very appropriateness of the term "religion," preferring instead to see this term as a "Western" imposition. Rather than regard religion as something internal to the individual, there is a preference to regard religion as a human creation, the site of various contestations and collaborations over ideas and terms that have been signified as divine or transcendent.

It should, hopefully, be quite clear how the insider/outsider problem fits within Jewish studies. For "insider" not only can refer to the desire to explain "religious" forms from the perspective of those who perform and believe in them but also be implicit when one engages in explanatory work, and at the same time, is a religious practitioner of the religion in question. The relationship between insiders and outsiders, however, is frequently bound up with larger theoretical issues. Does, for example, the insider who studies his or her religion present him- or herself as a metonym for the tradition? Does the insider become the resource from whom undergraduates of the same religious or ethnic persuasion can get advice? The potential—and I say potential because we should not make the simplistic claim that insiders are incapable of studying their own religion critically—problem with the insider approach is that the personal and by nature idiosyncratic beliefs and behaviors of the individual become largely untheorized (McCutcheon 2003, 345).

Heilman's comments that opened this chapter clearly reflect the biases of the insider. According to this account, the insider—based on his or her genetic, ethnic, or religious affiliation or attachment to the subject matter—possesses a unique access to the data in question. This is one of the major existential problems of both area studies and religious studies. They represent two of the primary academic fields in the human sciences in which the participant's own self-report, the so-called emic point of view, is given pride of place. In the majority of fields, by contrast, this point of view is treated as but an additional instance of data in need of theorization.

The insider point of view (whether of the practitioner, scholar, or practitioner-scholar), however, is predicated on reified notions of identity that, as I tried to argue above, are highly problematic. Jewish identity—whether in those we study or in ourselves—is not infrequently assumed to be stable and normative. The result is that the category "Judaism" is often untheorized, assumed to be a given, and, as a result, remains connected to the interests of those who define, circumscribe, and subsequently create the very category that they seek to find in the natural world (see Hughes 2010b). On this reading, an insider approach to Judaism is potentially more problematic than that of the outsider. Assuming that the outsider has no hostile (in the case of Jewish data, this can often mean supersessionist or "anti-Semitic") intent, his or her reading should ideally take precedence over the insider.

This perhaps sets up a false dichotomy. We should be careful of assuming that insiders are somehow rendered incompetent to function as scholars of their own tradition. In fact, as we shall see in the following chapter, one of the reasons that, since its inception as an academic discipline in the nineteenth century, Jews have been the primary scholars of their own tradition is because non-Jews were either uninterested in Jewish data (at least after the birth of Jesus) or so biased and prejudiced in their interpretations of Judaism as to make such analysis worthless. Jewish studies, in other words, has had a number of external (e.g., supersessionist, anti-Semitic, disinterested) and internal (e.g., identity politics) forces that, when combined, have created a discipline that is largely peopled by insiders.

The debate between Bird and Heilman, a variation on the age-old insider/outsider problem, takes us to the crux of many of the problems that beset Jewish studies as an academic field. Is it an advocacy unit on campus—functioning as a resource for Jewish students, rallying support for Israel, and addressing anti-Semitism if and when it rears its ugly head? Or is it but one among many academic disciplines, in which case the scholar of Jewish data maintains an objective distance from his or her data and seeks to find engaged and engaging conversation partners with fellow academics in cognate disciplines. Rather than be a resource for Jewish students, such a scholar may know nothing about the intricate halakhic (legal) rules and rituals of

Judaism and may even be a vociferous critic of Israel and its right-wing policies.

A related question is what is the role of the non-Jew in the Jewish studies classroom? Numerous individuals who support financially Jewish studies programs on campus are often surprised to learn that the majority of students in our classes (not to mention, those that often do the best) are non-Jews. This potentially creates a real problem (one to be examined in chapter 3): Why, so some reason, should such donors support fellowships in Jewish studies if they are going to non-Jewish students? Although questions such as these must, for now at least, remain theoretical, it is not hard to imagine their practical consequences for the academic study of Judaism. The great paradox of Jewish studies is that despite the majority of non-Jews who take Jewish studies classes, by graduate school virtually all students specializing in Jewish data in departments of religious studies, Jewish studies, or Near Eastern studies (often with the exception of those working in the Hebrew Bible/Old Testament) are Jews.

The debate between Heilman and Bird also reveals the tensions over what the goal of Jewish studies ought to be. Is it, as many believe, to show the Jewish contribution to Western civilization? The institution in which I used to teach (SUNY, Buffalo), for example, defines its mandate as "focused on teaching and scholarship related to the contributions of the Jewish tradition in the development of Western civilization." However, many others prefer to argue that we can never articulate "Jewish" ideas, let alone "Jewish" contributions, because such ideas always respond to and are in conversation with the "non-Jewish" civilizations in which Jews live. Rather than uphold reified borders between Jews and and non-Jews, borders that are often retrofitted and projected onto the past, some, myself included, argue that it might be more profitable to examine the fluidity between such terms (e.g., D. Boyarin 2004; Hughes 2010a, ix–xvii).

These are intractable debates. And it is certainly not my intention either to mediate or solve them in the pages that follow. On the contrary, my goal is to highlight them and show the various ways in which they pull the academic study of Judaism in different—often radically different—directions. In many ways, the problems besetting Jewish studies are not unlike those that other area studies programs face within the academy. Talk of a, let alone *the*, "Jewish" (or "Asian" or "female" or "Latin American" or "African American") experience is highly problematic and full of such essentialist baggage as to make it virtually useless.

Before proceeding, however, it might be worthwhile noting that despite the overwhelming fascination of all things Jewish within Jewish studies, there nevertheless remains, in certain circles, a healthy critical approach. That is, not everyone engaged within Jewish studies examines and analyzes his or her data in an apologist manner. Given its rather lengthy history of development (the subject matter of the following chapter), Jewish studies exhibits a surprisingly eclectic range of interests and fields. It cannot simply be ignored or passed over as an advocacy unit and keeper of the Zionist flame, although in some units and programs this may well be the case.

Between Semitism and Anti-Semitism: Religious Studies Confronts Its Inner Jew

Up to this point, I have examined the rather insular nature of Jewish studies, showing the isomorphic relationships among authenticity, identity, and scholarship. In the remaining part of this chapter, I switch focus and examine the role or trope of "Judaism" within the academic study of religion. For many theorists of religion, from Marx to Otto to Eliade, Judaism has functioned pejoratively, becoming as it were the foil against which their respective theories took shape. This connects to my larger argument in the chapter that one of the main reasons for the insularity of Jewish studies in the present has emerged though a complex set of internal and external variables, centripetal and centrifugal forces. When combined, these forces have created an apologetic tendency within Jewish studies, one that has remained there since its inception.

Jewish studies as an academic field both originated and took shape in Germany in the first half of the nineteenth century. Although some of the processes responsible for articulating this will be the subject of the following chapter, it should suffice to mention in the present context that the academic study of Judaism in this period was intertwined with much larger forces, such as anti-Semitism, the legal position of Jews within German society, and the larger issue of Jewish integration (Wiese 2005, 5). Despite the fact that many German orientalists were attracted to the exotic and "oriental" nature of the Old Testament, they did so with the aim of "delegitimizing rabbinic Hebrew and robbing modern Jews of special rights or skills in this endeavor" (Marchand 2009, 39). This is undoubtedly related to the larger context wherein "the Jew" has functioned as the quintessential

Other for much of Christian theological speculation since the time of Jesus (see Hughes 2010b), in addition to playing a negative role against which the creation of the modern nation-state in Europe, itself based on reified notions of racial and linguistic purity, took shape (e.g., Elon 2002; Steinweis 2008; and as a literary trope in Western culture, see the essays in Nochlin and Garb 1996).

A complete survey of the ways in which "Judaism" and "the Jew" have figured in European conceptions of religion in general and within the academic study of religion more particularly is beyond the scope of the present study. However, it is worth mentioning that the "Jewish Question" (Ger: "Judenfrage"; Fr: "la Question juive") was the name given to describe the negative attitude toward the apparent and persistent singularity of the Jews as a people against the background of rising political nationalisms. Many pamphlets, treatises, and monographs were put forth to address this "Jewish Question" with an eye toward solving it. Such solutions included assimilation, emancipation, national sovereignty, deportation, and most severe of all, ultimate extermination.

Karl Marx (1818–1883)—the German philosopher, radical socialist, and theorist of religion—although of Jewish descent, was highly critical of Judaism, a religious form that he associated with "hucksterism" (Marx 1844). The catalyst of Marx's treatise entitled "On the Jewish Question" was a treatise by the same name composed by Bruno Bauer (1843). Bauer argued that Jews could achieve political emancipation only if they relinquished their religion, which he believed to be incompatible with universal human rights. In response to Bauer, Marx differentiated between political emancipation—essentially the grant of liberal rights and liberties—and human emancipation. Whereas Bauer had argued that political emancipation is incompatible with religion (whether Judaism or Christianity), Marx argued that it was perfectly compatible with the continued existence of religion, as shown by the contemporary example of the United States. However, Marx went further and argued that political emancipation was insufficient to bring about human emancipation. Since the latter is based on the idea that each individual needs protection from other individuals, real freedom is to be found in human community, not in isolation, based on non-alienated labor (Wolff 2002, 14–37).

All is well and good, however, until Marx turns to his analysis of Judaism, which implies that the modern capitalist world is essentially the triumph of Judaism, a pseudoreligion whose god is money and exploitation:

Money is the jealous god of Israel, in face of which no other god may exist. Money abuses all the gods of man—and turns them into commodities. Money is the universal self-established *value* of all things. It has, therefore, robbed the whole world—both the world of men and nature—of its proper value. Money is the alienated essence of man's work and man's existence, and this alien essence dominates him, and he worships it. The god of the Jews has become secularized and has become the god of the world. The bill of exchange is the real god of the Jew. His god is only an illusory bill of exchange. (Marx 1844, 49)

As a result of this, Marx argues that society is *Jewish* and that everyone, including Jews and Christians, must be emancipated from it. He concludes his essay with the following: "The *social* emancipation of the Jew is the *emancipation of society from Judaism*" (1844, 51; his italics). That is, Judaism—synonymous with capitalism—has, for Marx, now become *the* problem facing all humanity. Liberation for society means transcending Judaism.

This is not the place to go into all the details of Marx's analysis of either Judaism or class warfare. It is the place, however, to note that Marx's reductionist view of religion has exercised a strong influence on the discipline of religious studies up to the present (e.g., Pals 1996, 124–57). Whether Marx is speaking metaphorically or polemically against Bauer in *The Jewish Question* is impossible to tell, but what is clearly on display is a highly anti-Semitic portrayal of Judaism as a religion of greed and selfishness that was in keeping with much conspiracy theory of the time and that was largely based on a set of perceived connections between Jews and world domination.[8] It is an opinion of Judaism, moreover, that even if not shared by the larger discipline of religious studies, nevertheless is present in one of its central theorists and one that has the potential to make this larger discipline rather exclusive of Jews and Judaism.

Another central figure in the development of religious studies is Rudolph Otto (1869–1937). Otto was a Protestant theologian at the University of Marburg's divinity school, and his best-known work is *The Idea of the Holy* (1958 [1917]).[9] Central to the work is what he describes as the experience of the holy, which he defines using the Latin term "numinous" as a mental state that "is perfectly *sui generis* and irreducible to any other; and therefore, like every absolutely primary and elementary datum, while it admits of being discussed, it cannot be strictly defined" (Otto 1958 [1917], 7). The numinous, then, is an experience that can be neither analyzed nor studied. It forms the root of religion and is in danger of being masked or corrupted by external forms such as prayer, liturgy, and ritual. Traditional religious expressions, in other words, represent rational and conscious expressions of what is otherwise an essentially irrational and unconscious feeling, something that forms the core of all religious expressions. This "numinous" feeling, what he sometimes refers to as "creaturely feeling" or "*mysterium tremendum*," he defines as a cross-cultural phenomenon.

Although fellow Christian theologians such as Karl Barth and Rudolf Bultmann would fault Otto for his focus on the irrational and his failure to characterize biblical revelation as unique, his thought and work can certainly be contextualized within the larger themes of contemporaneous Protestant theology (Alles 1996, 8–9). This theological context was one that had largely defined itself in opposition to the perceived excesses of Jewish legalism and Catholic ritualism. This legacy, according Robert Orsi and others, remains implicit, though rarely articulated, within the history of the academic study of religion—where the religion against which all others were compared (and, indeed, still are)—has been a "domesticated civic Protestantism" (Orsi 2005, 186). The result, according to Orsi, is that religious studies has been constructed largely by means of excluding those religious forms that threaten the order and stability of Protestantism: Judaism, Catholicism, Mormonism, Pentecostalism, among others, which have largely become "relegated to the world of sects, cults, fundamentalisms, popular piety, ritualism, magic, primitive religion, millennialism, anything but "religion" (Orsi 2005, 188).

Returning to Otto and his theory of the "numinous," it is perhaps no surprise that he locates the heart or essence of religion with an internal feeling of "awe" that is far removed from ritual or liturgy. These two latter concepts are among the defining elements of both Judaism and Catholicism. Otto—as was common in so much of theorizing about religion in the twentieth century—takes something that he feels (pun intended) to be an integral part of his own religion, transforms it into a cross-cultural concept, and then projects it onto the rest of the world's "religions." Otto's preference for his own religion is perhaps best witnessed, not in *The Idea of the Holy*, but in one of the other, many books that he wrote. In 1908, ten years before he published his magnum opus, he wrote a small book entitled *The Life and Ministry of Jesus, According to the Critical Method: Being a Course of Lectures*. Therein he writes of Jesus: "He possessed such an inner concentration, such an hierarchy of powers, such a consciousness of self and of God as were able to carry him victoriously through all the storms of life. Hence he had an inner certainty, a deep assurance, which profited in every condition and which made the plain Nazarene, the carpenter's son, superior to all the scribes, the high priests, and the Roman Procurator. He was an upright, resplendent, genuine, free-born and a truly kingly being" (Otto 1908, 82–83). Here, Otto shows Jesus' superiority to the "scribes and the high priests," which functions as fairly obvious code for the Jewish leadership at the time of Jesus. Once again, then, we are on fairly firm supersessionist terrain: Jesus transcended the religious forms of his day and in so doing became a beacon of love to the world, offering a "teaching [that] was comprehensible to the plainest man and, at the same time, full of infinite matter to the deepest" (Otto 1908, 84). Otto's predilection for his own tradition and its access to the "numinous," for example, indicated the numinous manifests in its fullest form within the (protestant) Christian faith (178).

Although not nearly as anti-Semitic as the work of Marx, we nevertheless again see how an early twentieth-century theorist of religion virtually ignores Judaism and Jewish data, except of course for the Old Testament. This ignorance, though, is not simply predicated on a lack of knowledge of Judaism, but based on the lengthy Christian concept of supersessionism. Judaism is not mentioned because implicit is the notion that it is barely a "religion" (in the sense of access to the numinous) and has been spiritually surpassed by Christianity, which can offer spiritual access to all.

Mircea Eliade (1907–1986) was one of the most important theoreticians of religious studies in the twentieth century. He probably did more than anyone in the United States to popularize the academic study of religion, and he was responsible for training a generation of scholars at the divinity school at the University of Chicago. Since his death, however, his legacy has been largely thrown into disrepute owing to his essentialism, lack of historicism (see, e.g., Smith 1978, 253–59), and youthful involvement with and support for Romania's profascist and anti-Semitic Iron Guard (see, e.g., Strenski 1987, 92–103; Dubuisson 2006).[10] Some contend that the latter support for fascism made its way into his theory of religion, which was predicated on the notion that true, authentic religious experience takes pace in the countryside among rural or "archaic" people (e.g., Berger 1994, 51–74; Dubuisson 2006, 189–208).

In his desire to construct a "morphology of the sacred" (Eliade 1958, 7–14), Eliade is quick to differentiate between what he calls "*homo religiosus*" and "modern man." The former, often romantically

conceived of as a peasant whose existence is imbued with folk customs handed down through the centuries, is contrasted with deni-
zens of cities, those whose lives are characterized by the absence or
displacement of the so-called "sacred." In a striking juxtaposition
between these two types of individuals, Eliade argues,

> Religious man assumes a particular and characteristic mode
> of existence in the world. . . . Whatever the historical context
> in which he is placed *homo religiosus* always believes that
> there is an absolute reality, *the sacred*, which transcends this
> world but manifests itself in this world, thereby sanctifying
> it and making it real . . . [N]onreligious man refuses tran-
> scendence, accepts the relativity of "reality," and may even
> come to doubt the meaning of existence . . . [H]e refuses
> all appeals to transcendence. (1959, 202–203)

Without getting into the obvious problems with such ontological
essentialism and the ambiguous use of the term "sacred," Eliade is
here mistrustful of the pull of history (which removes *homo religiosus*
from his or her experience with the sacred) and the city, which contributes to this displacement. Keeping in mind Eliade's commitment
to and support for Romanian fascism, his mistrust of the city—in
Eastern European folklore, the home of "the money-lending Jews"—
can be read in counterpoint with the countryside, the locus of pure
Romanian *Volkreligion*.

Unlike the world of nature, which functions as the locus of
the sacred, Eliade argues that the city exacerbates the dislocation of
modernity. Eliade, thus, seems to be working with the traditional
romantic stereotype that argues that cities are places of sin, corruption,
and greed; whereas it is only in the countryside that one encounters
authentic forms of religious expression (Orsi 1999, 3–13). Implicit here
is the assumption that city life is frantic, frenetic and unstable, a place
of moral depravity where different religions and ethnic groups bump
against one another and mix and mingle. The result is that city life
is traditionally characterized as a place of alienation, of strangeness,
and of inauthenticity. Rural life, on the other hand, is associated with
simplicity and a purity of place, where concepts such as multiculturalism and complex religious forms are absent. Rural life and peasant
religion is an intersection of wholeness and of authenticity.

Although many claim that nothing anti-Semitic can be found in
Eliade's postwar writings, it seems quite clear that his tidy distinctions between the sacrality of religion and the profanity of history,

and between rural simplicity or authenticity and urban complexity can easily be read in such a manner that problematizes Jews and Judaism. Judaism, for example, is traditionally held up as the historical religion par excellence because it conceives of God as an actor in history. Moreover, as mentioned above, Jews were notorious for their urban existence in Europe. Also telling is the fact that Eliade, for the most part, largely ignored postbiblical forms of Judaism.

∼

These three portraits provide a window onto the larger world of religious studies. They reveal, moreover, that the discipline has not necessarily been the most hospitable place for the study of Judaism or Jewish data. Whether reflected in Marx's criticism of religion, Otto's desire to focus on a nonritualized inner experience or Eliade's valorization of the authenticity of the sacred, it seems safe to conclude that Judaism has been ill served by much of the classic and influential religious studies theorizing in the twentieth century.[11] The history of Christian supersessionism coupled with the rise of anti-Semitism in Europe in the late nineteenth and early twentieth centuries cannot, on fundamental levels, be separated from the emergence of the academic study of religion. "The Jew" as the quintessential Other and Judaism frequently described in Pauline terms as a "non-religion" or a "legalistic" religion have meant that Jewish data has not always been accepted at face value within the larger discipline of the academic study of religion in the modern world.

Conclusions: Situating Judaism

This chapter has focused on some of the centripetal and centrifugal forces at work in situating Judaism within religious studies. Judaism's place within this larger disciplinary unit is neither obvious nor straightforward. The study of Judaism's propensity for insidership and the study of religion's tendency toward excluding Judaism, as I have suggested in this chapter, most likely represent two sides of the same coin. Without casting blame, it seems that the academic study of religion's emphasis on Protestant religious forms (which are, in turn, assumed to be of cross-cultural relevance) and the Old Testament (including its fulfillment in the New) has not served the analysis of Judaism well. Judaism stands too close to the formation of Christianity, and this has meant that the former has tended to be marginalized within the academic study of religion, a discipline predicated on the terms and categories of the latter. This has, in large part, contributed to the insular nature of much of Jewish studies. At the same time, however, Jewish studies cannot use this past simply as a way to dismiss engagement with the academic study of religion.

The academic study of Judaism, much like the study of every religion, has a history peculiar to it, one that is largely based on Christianity's encounter with it. Because Judaism has always loomed large in the Christian imagination, functioning as the Other against which Christian theologians have both defined and imagined themselves and their tradition, it should come as little surprise that a particular version of Judaism—as rigid, as legalistic, as spiritually impoverished—has always been present in Christianity. As the academic study of religion began to separate itself from theology by turning to history and other disciplines in the late nineteenth and early twentieth centuries, however, this pejorative version of Judaism has nevertheless tended to remain as a silent partner.

But this is the way things have been. It is not necessarily the way things are at the present moment. While the Protestant assumptions of what religion is and what sort of work it performs still largely color the discipline, surely enough critical work has been done in recent decades to point out religious studies' crypto-theological agenda and its latent supersessionism and even anti-Semitism (e.g., Strenski 1987, 104–128; McCutcheon 1997; Lincoln 1999; Dubuisson 2003). This is what makes the ethnocentrism with which I began this chapter potentially so disturbing.

The origins of the academic study of Judaism revolve around issues of identity, anti-Semitism, and the fight for civic and legal equality. This may well account for the propensity toward insularity that we still witness to this day within certain trajectories of the discipline. In order to explore this in greater detail, it is necessary to turn attention to the origins of the academic study of Judaism in nineteenth-century Germany.

2

Encountering Tradition

The Search for a Jewish Essence

The previous chapter attempted to provide a general overview of some of the problems and possibilities associated with the modern academic encounter with Judaism. My principle concern, to reiterate, is with the interface between Judaism and religious studies, the larger unit in which the study of Judaism is customarily housed for various administrative and ideological reasons. The Bird/Heilman controversy functioned as a window through which to glimpse upon the complex intersection between authenticity, identity, and scholarship. The tension between the insider and the outsider, and how this relates to the larger issue of who possesses the authority to study Jewish data, as this controversy so poignantly reminds us, remains at the center of how Judaism is both imagined and situated. Perhaps the natural question to ask at this stage of the analysis is: How did things get this way? Why is it that, for the most part, Jews primarily teach Jewish studies at colleges and universities?[1] In order to begin the process of answering this and related questions, it is first necessary to inquire into the origins of the academic study of Judaism. When did it begin, for example, and what were the various material and intellectual contexts that produced it?

Discovering Jewish History

From its origins in the nineteenth century, the academic study of Judaism has largely been bound up with the apologetical desire to show that Jews and Judaism were normal. From its inception, we see that the study of Judaism has not necessarily been an academic enterprise, but primarily an existential and a political one. This is significant because, prior to the application of academic approaches to Judaism, both rabbinic chosenness and Christian supersessionism had tended, albeit for different reasons, to deny Judaism a history (Yerushalmi 1989, 84–87). Whereas the former located Judaism's superiority in a set of timeless and sacred texts (e.g., Bible, Talmud), the latter sought to show its inferiority with the claim that after the advent of Jesus, Jews possessed neither a history nor a territory. Land, power, and providence—it is important to remember—were intimately connected to one another: to lack one was necessarily to lack the others. The fact that Jews possessed neither a home nor any political or other power could be and was connected to the later anti-Semitic notion that Jewish existence was parasitic, needing other nations and languages to sustain it. Not surprisingly, then, history, and its use of rhetoric and methods, became an important tool for both those who wanted to claim that Jews did indeed possess a history (and, thus, were normal) and for those who wanted to deny such claims.

Those Jewish thinkers responsible for this new understanding of Judaism, writes Leora Batnitsky, did not so much secularize Judaism as redefine the tradition as a religion (2011, 36). That is, the individuals to be discussed below sought to mold Judaism into a set of claims that could easily fit within the modern, Protestant category of religion. Since Judaism was historically based on law and practice, it was largely public in nature and, as such, intersected with cultural, political, social, and legal concerns. This did not square, however, with the notion that religion was something private, an inner experience that had to be articulated and defined in terms of faith and belief. The nineteenth century was a time, then, in which Jewish scholars/ reformers sought to make Jews normal by transforming Judaism into a religion in this Protestant and European sense of the term.

Before examining the rise of Jewish studies, which contributed greatly to this redefinition of Judaism, it might be worthwhile to make a few comments about the origins of our modern discipline of history (*Geschichte*). This discipline is largely the invention of the nineteenth-century German university. This period, for example, witnessed the creation of histories of nations produced by German nationalist historians such as Johann Gustav Droysen (1808–1884), Heinrich Karl Ludolf von Sybel (1817–1895), and Heinrich Gotthard von Treitschke (1834–1896). Such individuals, in both the service and employment of the state, used history as a way to imagine and shape national identity. This is certainly not to imply that history did not exist before this time period; however, it is to make the claim that the tools and methods used to discover it and the narrative techniques imagined to frame and disseminate it emerged only with the rise of the modern university. Within this context, it is important to remember that the primary social function of the university was connected to the rise of nationalism and the creation of a class of intellectuals to disseminate nationalist ideology (see, for example, the studies in Ringer 1969, Craig 1984).

History, as conceived by early theorists such as J. G. Herder and J. Fichte, was intimately connected to the fate of nations (Iggers 1983, 1–10). For such individuals, the goal of the historical record was to "relate the existence of discrete national organisms, each operating according to its idiosyncratic laws of development" (Myers 1995, 13). History accordingly played a key role in both imagining and forging together a national community. Imagined by professional scholars in the nineteenth century, historical research was not simply a form of cold or disinterested research (even though this is precisely how it was often portrayed), but a quest for national glory and self-recognition. This often involved locating a pristine past that could function as the vehicle for contemporary regeneration.

The "discovery" of Jewish history, perhaps not surprising given the fact that Jews adopted the theoretical methods and models produced by the likes of Herder and Fichte, coincided with the "discovery" of the histories and national identities of various European states. Much like their non-Jewish colleagues were doing for the glory of their own nations, Jewish intellectuals sought to create and forge an identity for Jews using the tools that the discipline of history provided them. This meant trying to create a Jewish Volk independent of rabbinic claims that Jews existed outside of history owing to their chosenness and anti-Semitic claims to deny such a history because Jews lacked a state of their own. The rise of Jewish history was, in many ways, an apologetical enterprise, one that both responded to and took place against a complex backdrop of religious reform, political emancipation, and anti-Semitism. Many young Jews, both alienated from and fed up with the traditional forms of religious education, began to enter German universities, and therein they began to study classics, history, philology, philosophy, and Semitic languages. Although allowed to attend universities and receive university degrees, Jews were prevented from holding academic positions as long as they remained Jews. To enter the professoriate, one first had to be a Christian.

The first generation of university-trained Jewish historians formed themselves into a society that they called Verein für Kultur und Wissenscahft der Juden, "The Society for the Culture and Science of the Jews." Formed against the backdrop of a strong conservative tide in Prussia and other German states following the defeat of Napoleon, it provided these individuals with a place to read papers to one another and discuss the complex relationship of Jews to larger German society (Schorsch 1994, 221–23). The group met for the first time in Berlin in November 1819 with the explicit aim of applying critical historical scholarship to Jewish sources. Their vision was not simply academic, but political: Jewish self-improvement through scholarship would ideally lead to full political emancipation. Their desire to implement this vision was revolutionary. They desired nothing less than a new conception of Judaism, one that could be historicized as a religious civilization and one that, reconfigured, would lead to reform within the tradition and political emancipation for it from without. And for the next five years, these "disaffected visionaries" struggled to develop a program for an emancipated Judaism, one that ultimately met with very little success, according to Schorsch, on account of "their unfavorable social status, their fiercely intellectual bent, and their impervious elitism" (Schorsch 1994, 206).[2]

Leopold Zunz and Wissenschaft des Judentums

One of the key figures in the Verein was Leopold Zunz (1794–1886), who received a doctorate from the University of Halle and was later ordained as a Reform rabbi (requisite biographical information may be found in Schorsch 1994, 242–48). In 1818, Zunz published what would amount to a manifesto of the new movement that came to be known as Wissenschaft des Judentums (the "scientific study of Judaism"), the genealogical precursor to the modern and anglicized "Jewish studies." The essay, entitled *"Etwas über die rabbinische Literatur"* ("On Rabbinic Literature"), provided one of the earliest attempts to apply the canons of Western scholarship to Judaism.[3] It set out to establish a new set of secular, intellectual categories to write about Judaism, leading to a new conceptualization of both Jews and their role in history. According to Zunz, the Hebrew Bible has been transformed "into a structure of spiritual industry more wondrous even than the Greek, for its richness was created from a more sanctified matter. Such an appreciation was never granted to the later productions of the Hebrew nation" (Zunz 1995 [1873], 221). Zunz set out to correct this oversight and, in the process, attempted to overcome the widespread neglect of Jewish literature subsequent to the Bible. He found this especially disconcerting at a time "when all science and all of man's doings have been illumined in brilliant rays, when the remote corners of the earth have been reached, the most obscure languages studied and nothing seems too insignificant to assist in the construction of wisdom, how is it possible that our science [i.e., the academic study of rabbinic literature] alone lies neglected" (Zunz 1995 [1873], 222)? To rectify matters, Zunz called for the presentation of the entire literature of the Jews "as the object of scholarly research" (Zunz 1995 [1873], 222). At a time when the academic world was interested in investigating any and every subject, he argues, it has systematically ignored the form and contents of rabbinic literature. The primary reason for this, as he will mention later in the essay, has nothing to do with the contents of this literature, but is largely the result of prejudice on the part of Christian scholars. In focusing his attention on rabbinic literature, Zunz himself purposefully ignored biblical literature, claiming that it was already too well known by the non-Jewish world. Instead, Zunz sought to use the academic tools supplied by non-Jewish scholarship that he had learned at German universities to create in a systematic fashion a Jewish renaissance that would, in his own words, witness the creation of "critical editions of manuscripts, good translations, accurate reference works, biographies and the like" (Zunz 1995 [1873], 223).

By applying the canons of scholarship provided by such disciplines as philology and classical literature, Zunz sought to reveal the literary heritage produced by Jews after the closure of the Bible. This was, to reiterate, revolutionary. For one thing, Zunz sought to dislodge rabbis from their traditional role as the self-described "guardians" of such texts. The proper place to study these texts was no longer in the yeshiva (rabbinic seminary), but in a secular and academic setting under the tutelage of university-trained scholars. In addition, the systematic and scholarly presentation of these texts would reveal to non-Jews that the texts produced by Jews in the rabbinic period were on par intellectually with those produced by non-Jews.

Zunz's manifesto called for an investigation into and taxonomy of "rabbinic literature," a term he used in a very wide-ranging and inclusive sense. This literature would, in the words of Schorsh, exhibit "the vast expanse of literature written in Hebrew by literate laymen as well as practicing rabbis that matched all the literary genres of a living people" (Schorsch 1994, 221). The goal of this was to begin the process of reforming the tradition, the first step in the process of political emancipation. It fell to the scholar to "recognize and distinguish among the old and the useful, the obsolete and the harmful, the new and the desirable, we must embark upon a considered study of the people and its political and moral history" (Zunz 1995 [1873], 222). This scholarship, in other words, was not disinterested. It played a crucial role in determining what was essential and useful. If it was found to be such, then it should remain; concomitantly, that deemed inconsequential or tangential would not be considered of value and, thus, a candidate for removal. These decisions, of course, were highly ideological and idiosyncratic. It became part of the job description of the secular scholar of Jewish texts to decide what part of the tradition to keep and what to throw out. Zunz's desire was to displace the contemporary version of rabbinic Judaism, something he felt held little in common with its Talmudic and medieval precursors. In his words, "rabbanism as presently constituted is a decadent institution of ignorance, arrogance and fanaticism, diametrically opposed to the better efforts of some Jews and the humanitarian measures of the government" (qtd. in Schorsch 1994, 213).

A subsequent generation of scholars took up Zunz's challenge and began the process of filling in his initial vision. In his massive eleven-volume *History of the Jews* (1853–1876), for example, Heinrich Graetz (1817–1891), one of the founders of modern Jewish history, attempted to write a universal history of Jews, one that attempted to distill the essence of "the Jewish people," showing its various historical manifestations. Around the ninth and tenth centuries, Graetz writes that a major transformation occurred in the history of Jewish communities: "We turn gladly from the decay of the internal organization of the East to the vitality of the communities in the Guadalquiver and the Guadiana. Vigorous forces and spiritual currents of a most varied character asserted themselves everywhere, and produced the brilliant efflorescence of Jewish culture. There arose in the Jewish communities of Andalusia intense zeal for the various branches of knowledge, and an eager desire for creative activity" (Graetz 1956, 235). Here Graetz contrasts the decay of the East, and with it Oriental Jewry,[4] with the rise of the West and European Jews in Spain. Only these European Jews are "European" in the sense that contemporaneous Europeans were not. Whereas Graetz characterizes the latter as "shameless rabble," a "bloodthirsty people," a "violent mob," "degenerate Crusaders," and so on, Jews are motivated by "creativity," "spirituality," and a "zeal" for knowledge. In another passage, Graetz—in his typical desire to associate intellectual trends and changes in individuals—locates this transmission from Orient to Occident in the figure of Hasdai ibn Shaprut (ca. 915–ca. 970), who "was quite modern in his character, entirely different from the type of his predecessors. His easy, pliant, and genial nature was free both from the heaviness of the Orientals and the gloomy earnestness of the Jews. His actions and expressions make us look upon him as a European, and through him, so to speak, Jewish history receives a European character" (Graetz 1956, 215–16). This "European" nature of Jews, stretching back at least until the ninth century, provided contemporary Jews with a noble genealogy, a pedigree, as Schorsch has well demonstrated (1995, 71–92), that sought to guarantee Jews equality in the modern period. Graetz writes that, like Wissenschaft scholars of his own generation, these great scholars of the past "were not narrow specialists . . . if not poets themselves, they found pleasure in the rhythmic compositions of the new Hebrew poesy . . . The prominent men, who, either through their political position or their merits stood at the head of Jewish affairs in Spain, were for the most part noble characters imbued with the highest sentiments. . . . Their religious life was elevated and idealized through this higher culture" (Graetz 1956, 235–236). Here Graetz attempts to uncover the *mentalité* of the past. These men (and, of course, they were never interested in women) possessed aesthetic and rational sensibilities that were "imbued with the highest sentiments." They were religious, but their religious motivations were not fanatical, but informed by the "higher culture" that they produced. Untouched by the obscurantism and flights of fancy of kabbalah or Jewish mysticism, these medieval rationalists could be constructed as either "just like us" or those to whom we should aspire to be. In his 1878 history of the Jewish people, Samuel Bäck (1834–1912) writes that these Spanish Jews

> cultivated all areas of intellectual activity and nevertheless maintained a steadfast fidelity to their religion; they observed every statute that the Bible and the Talmud prescribed, and never forgot that they were Jews. These Spanish Jews occupied the highest state offices and yet also adhered lovingly to Judaism; these Jewish scholars immersed themselves in the depths of philosophy and were also familiar with the most secret branches of the Talmud. Jewish physicians, travelers, and merchants maintained a love and zeal for Jewish scholarship. (Bäck 1906, 264)

Graetz, Bäck, and others subsequently contrasted this nobility of culture and character with the general dearth of both in Christian Europe. Indeed Graetz implies that it was the medieval Jews of Spain and their diaspora that saved philosophy and reintroduced it to Europe: "A Christian Emperor destroyed the temple of philosophy in Athens, and exiled its last priests. Since that time philosophy had been outlawed in Europe; at least, it was little known there, and had been compelled to find a home in Asia. The Jewish thinker Ibn Gabirol, was the first to transplant it again to Europe, and he built an altar to it in Spain, where it found a permanent habitation" (Graetz 1956, 270). This led Moritz Steinschneider (1816–1907), another central figure of the Wissenschaft movement, to argue that bringing this rational past to light was not just a Jewish activity, but should also be a pan-European one. For the likes of Steinschneider, it was the German state, and not traditional Jewish institutions, that had a large role to play in providing the support necessary to uncover Jewish history and ideas, and their contribution to European civilization. He writes,"The state and its scientific institutions must foster scientific investigations of the Jewish works contained in their libraries, just as they are investigating the pyramids, the ruins of Pompeii and of Nineveh. They should do this all the more so since the spirit which has created these works has not yet died out, but is still alive in the citizens of their state" (Steinschneider 1869, 76). Like his contemporary Graetz, Steinschneider argues that the greatness of the Jewish past is not some minor achievement, but among the greatest inheritances from the premodern world. It is, moreover, a discovery in the present that must be supported and cultivated. On par with the great archeological finds of Pompeii, Athens, and Rome, the Jewish past contributes to the betterment of all German society. Implicit in the above passage is that this "contribution" might be even more important because the spirit driving the Jewish past is not confined to dead monuments, but is alive and well in contemporary Judaism, *when properly understood*. Moreover, unlike the treasures of those ancient sites, the greatness of Judaism lies not in its physical monuments erected to various gods and goddesses, but in its aniconism and its textualism—two hallmark features of European civilization (Bland 2001, 13–20).

Finding Judaism's Essence: Unlocking the Past

Much Jewish scholarship in these early years was concerned with improving the lot of Jews. If Jews could be made to be more "European" in the sense that they, too, were seen to possess an essence and a history, they could be emancipated. The history of the Jews, retrofitted from the vantage point of the present, was now brought into existence. It was reified, studied, periodized, taxonomized, and its

defining elements extracted by means of a set of technical skills out-
lined in Zunz's essay (e.g., philology, text criticism, historiography).
Yet, once brought into existence, it began to do real ontological work.
Those aspects, as we have seen, that were deemed as enlightened,
aesthetic, and rational took pride of place in shaping the contours
of the past, and those aspects considered to be infelicitous, such as
the mystical and the obscurantist, were largely, as Scholem would
later argue (1971 and 1997), ignored and subsequently left out of the
authoritative canon of the Jewish past.

    Despite the cloak of scientific objectivity, giving Jews and Juda-
ism a history was largely motivated by both the necessity and the
urgency of political emancipation (Schorsch 1994, 163; Brenner 2010,
27–36). While it would certainly be a mistake to assume that the ever
expanding circle of Wissenschaft scholars represented a monolithic
school or program of research, the overwhelming majority shared a
belief in a larger project that the secular study of religious texts—
making critical editions of them, translating them, contextualizing
them—could facilitate such emancipation. Their use of history and
other scholarly methods was both chronistic in the sense that they
desired to produce a past and anachronistic in that they sought to
uncover a latent present, the seeds for future renewal, in that past.
In doing this, however they differed little from the means and ends
of non-Jewish scholars.

    The academic study of Judaism, thus, had its origins in a highly
charged political environment and consequently emerged as an apologetical enterprise. Scholarship was used to discover and unlock, or
alternatively unlock and discover, an essence of Judaism that fitted
well with the larger European context in which these scholars found
themselves. Located in the historical record, as opposed to a timeless
and authoritative set of religious texts, it was the job of the historian to manipulate the disciplines of history and philology to bring
this essence to light. Moreover, once unlocked, this essence could be
used to articulate a path toward future renewal. This idea of a Jewish "essence" played a crucial role in some of the earliest attempts to
write Jewish history. The discovery of this essence, after all, permitted
the perception of continuity in Jewish history (Schorsch 1994, 268).

    In order to explore this theme briefly, let me highlight how the
"essence" of Judaism plays out in the work of two of the best known
historians from the period in question: Abraham Geiger (1810–1874)
and the aforementioned Heinrich Graetz. Although differing in tone,
temperament, and the meaning they located in Jewish history, they
nevertheless shared a common assumption that Judaism possesses

an internal structure and that although this structure manifests itself most clearly in the historical record, it cannot be reduced to it.

Abraham Geiger, not coincidentally also one of the founding fathers of the Reform movement, wrote in the introduction to his *Das Judenthum und seine Geschichte* ("Judaism and Its History"), published between 1865 and 1871, that religion is not based on a dry legalism (i.e., that associated with rabbinic Judaism), but a spirit that animates humans to attain the nobler and loftier things in life:

> Religion may present itself in various outward forms; Religion, as such, is a necessity, the noblest attribute of man; it will cease only *with* man, not among men. As long as the spirit longeth after the Spirit of All, as long as this shall remain, so long shall religious life exist. Religion is life, all actions of man, if prompted by, and tending toward higher principles, are the work of Religion, are the result of Religion. Religion will become purer, more enlightened, but it will ever remain in existence, because man's longing and imperfection will never cease. (Geiger 1985, 22–23)

Geiger here speaks not of a particularistic "Judaism," but of a universal "religion," and indeed much of his life's work was motivated by his desire to detangle Judaism from what he considered to be outmoded notions such as peoplehood, ethnicity, and legalism. He defines religion as enlightened, pure, even rational, and only those aspects of Judaism that correspond to such features constitute its true and inner meaning. Not surprisingly, Geiger locates Judaism's essence in its refined notion of ethical monotheism,[5] the "idea of the unity and sanctity of God" (Geiger 1985, 211), a principle that was constantly under threat in Judaism's lengthy history; under threat, for example, by "the pretentious influence of a privileged priest-caste and an atoning sacrificial service" in the biblical period (Geiger 1985, 211). This ability of Judaism to cleanse and purify itself from within and to reach an inner equilibrium between freedom of interpretation and scriptural past came under especial threat in the Talmudic period when people "believed that they must cling to the past and all its peculiarities" (Geiger 1985, 235). This "time of ruin" severed the past from its creative interpretation, according to Geiger, and ushered in a period of intellectual slavery to the "letter of the law" (Geiger 1985, 238–39). Juxtaposed against this legal stagnation, Geiger imagined the rationality and creativity of the medieval Jewish philosophical tradition, a tradition that represented the synthesis between the two currents that defined Western civilization: "Whenever intellectual culture is about to begin a new flight, whenever the endeavor is renewed to advance from the plane of naïve consideration to a higher point of view, the students lean upon two ancient cultured nations and avail themselves of their literatures; namely the Hebrew and the Greek. Different in their points of view, Hebraism and Hellenism mutually supplement each other" (Geiger 1985, 300). Contact with the category of the so-called "non-Jewish," Geiger here implies, opens up the "Hebraic" creatively and meaningfully to its surrounding intellectual milieux. Geiger, in other words, sees two antithetic and mutually exclusive strains of medieval Jewish culture: the one, introspective and focused on the rigid interpretation of a fixed text, and the other critical of such an overreliance on legalism and, concomitantly, open to an intellectually vibrant interpretation of Judaism, one in tune with ancient Israel's monotheistic heritage. The latter for him is authentic, whereas the former is somehow a corruption.

Many were critical of Geiger's "Reform"-minded approach to Jewish history, especially his disregard of all that did not neatly fit with his model.[6] Heinrich Graetz, generally regarded as the ablest of the Wissenschaft historians, wrote his own version of Jewish history to counter that of Geiger. For him, Judaism was comprised not of a simple essence, but of a complex of religious and political factors. In his philosophy of Jewish history, *Die Konstruktion der jüdischen Geschichte* (The Structure of Jewish History), published in 1846, he argues that, unlike the Reform theory of Jewish history proposed by Geiger, earlier periods are never completely transcended, but, fugue-like, recur in later ones: "We are driven to conclude that Judaism has a religious character. Precisely this twofoldness characterizes the nature of Judaism. Knowledge of God and social welfare, religious truth and political theory form the two components of Judaism that are destined to flow through history thoroughly mixed" (Graetz 1975, 71). This "dual essence" permitted Graetz to argue that Judaism possessed its own unique history and that it could be co-opted neither by Reform agendas nor by Christian supersessionism. Once understood, it became clear to him that Judaism did not possess the customary "dark ages" of other civilizations. Whereas other civilizations ebbed and flowed between barbarism and higher forms of culture, Judaism has remained the same throughout its lengthy history (although with different cultural manifestations through the ages). He consequently saw it as his goal to "present [Jewish history's] tenacious and indestructible character, to prove that *Jewish history reveals no Middle Ages in the pejorative sense of the word*, that, in fact, the apparent state of death of Jewish history in the darkest days of the Middle Ages was merely an assumed disguise to escape from bloodthirsty brutality, or even a healthy, invigorating winter sleep, which fitted Judaism to enter into a daring, universal race against a more fortunate, younger opponent" (Graetz 1975, 94; my italics). The medieval period, on Graetz's reading, was not a period of stagnation, as it was for example in Christianity, but a time of inwardness and introspection, seeking to "explain itself in a mediated and theoretical manner" (Graetz 1975, 95). This was most clearly on display for Graetz in the medieval Jewish philosophical tradition that culminated in Maimonides' *Guide of the Perplexed* and "what formerly had occupied intellectuals in the quiet isolation of their study, now broke out in the open, stirred the people and became a catalyst of Jewish history" (Graetz 1975, 118).

Common to both Geiger's and Graetz's constructions of Jewish history was the desire to make Judaism rational, both to themselves and to their readers. Yet, as these two figures clearly reveal, this desire to write *the* history of *the* Jews was intimately bound up with modern concerns. The developmental structures that they located in Jewish history coincided with their own vision of what Judaism should be. Despite their radical intellectual differences concerning the essence and structure of Judaism, both sought to explain—or, perhaps better, translate—Judaism into the language and conceptual categories supplied by the non-Jewish world. This desire to shape Judaism using "foreign" and historical categories would, not surprisingly, meet with significant opposition from numerous quarters since it contradicted much of what Judaism and the Jewish people were traditionally thought to be. It should be clear, though, that the origins of the academic study of Judaism, including its formative years, were created in an ideological battle over the quiddity of Judaism. Jews undertook to study their past in these formative years primarily out of self-interest.

The battleground in all of these debates was the historical record—how it should be constructed and what it should include—and who possessed the authority to interpret it. Although I shall discuss the repercussions of this history of the history of Judaism in the following chapters, suffice it to say here that we encounter the origins of the introspective and insular nature of contemporary Jewish studies. Much of the framework for how the "Jewish past" ought to be constructed—including the notion that there is some sort of essence animating it and that it is retrievable in the textual or historical record—still largely animates the academic study of Judaism in the present. The sense of mission and the desire to defend Judaism from the attacks of non-Jews played a formative role in the disciplinary formation of Jewish studies, and it is one that seems—whether consciously or unconsciously—to have remained at the heart of Jewish studies into the present.

Cohen, Rosenzweig, and the Rejection of Jewish History

Not all German Jewish thinkers believed that history and the historical record represented the path to emancipation for European Jews. The Jewish critique of historicism in the late nineteenth century certainly cannot be removed from the larger German and European critique (Myers 2003, 30–34). The relativism and the cold distance afforded by historical method reflected what some considered to be the broader malaise of modernity, which displaced God as a historical agent in addition to traditional forms of religion. The growing backlash against history and historicism in certain quarters meant that some turned to other explanatory frameworks of the past. For all intents and purposes, there arose a prolonged and huge existential debate in Europe between faith and history. This debate is perhaps best symbolized by the revised publication in the 1860s of David Friedrich Strauss' *The Life of Jesus* (see the discussion in Myers 2003, 8–12). Strauss argued in this work that Jesus' life ought to be understood historically as opposed to mythically. Although it was one thing to employ historical methods to study, for example, the history and literature of the ancient Greeks, it was quite another to apply such methods to sacred scripture and the life of Jesus. The debates that erupted over the historical Jesus, in other words, revolved around the problem of history and historical method, and these debates became increasingly central, pitting historians against theologians throughout Europe.

Such debates certainly left their mark on Jewish scholars of the time. Many German-Jewish scholars, as we have seen, were drawn to history as a tool for religious change and political emancipation. These scholars, many associated with the fledgling denominations, frequently made appeals to history to determine what was essential and what was not. A new generation arose that was increasingly mistrustful of the historiographical arrogance or hubris of the likes of Geiger and Graetz. Many of this new generation were resistant to the prevailing norm that sought to justify Judaism according to its history.

Whereas earlier generations had taken great pains to show that Judaism and Jews were just like other nations, a new set of Jewish intellectuals increasingly questioned such correspondences. Instead they began to argue the more traditional perspective of the uniqueness of Judaism, going so far as to argue that Judaism "was a force that did not submit to the dictates of historical contingency" (Myers 2003, 31), although it was initially scholars associated with the more traditionally constructed denomination of Orthodox Judaism who initially called attention to the perceived excesses of history. (Recall that historicism was primarily the method that Reform- and Conservative-minded thinkers employed). Samson Raphael Hirsch (1808–1888), one of the major thinkers responsible for articulating Orthodox positions in contradistinction to Reform Judaism, argued, for example, in the first issue of *Jeschurun*, a journal that he founded in 1854, that Jews must necessarily accept the truth of biblical phrases such as "And God spoke to Moses": "so we must hold to it, fulfill it, without shortcuts or finding fault, in all circumstances and at all times. The Divine Word must reign eternal over all human judgment and we and all our deeds must be shaped by it. Instead of complaining that it is no longer suitable to the times, we should recognize only one legitimate complaint: that the times are no longer suitable to the Divine Word" (qtd. in Myers 2003, 31). For Hirsch, the eternality of the Divine Word, existing outside of the vagaries of historical existence, cannot be reduced to it. On the contrary, Judaism stands outside of the historical record, providing a beacon, as it were, that offers this record both meaning and sustenance.

While certainly one of the main bastions against historical critique, Orthodoxy was not the only position that sought to protect Judaism from the reductionist gaze of historicism. In this regard, one of the most important philosophical critics of Judaism as a historical force was Hermann Cohen (1842–1918), one of the founders of the neo-Kantian school at the University of Marburg and a former student of Heinrich Graetz. For Cohen, both Judaism's relevance and its superiority resided in its prophetic tradition. This tradition, to use Cohen's own language in his posthumously published *Religion of Reason: Out of the Sources of Judaism*, cannot be reduced to the historical:

> The history of religion has no means whatever of securing the legitimacy of religion; according to its own methodological concepts, there is no other legitimation for religion than that represented in the historical fact of religion. History thus surrenders the problem of discovering a concept of religion not only to the uncertainties of a more or less exhaustive compilation but also, in full accord with its own systematic tendency, to the possible results of induction, with all the latter's broadness and ambiguity. The concept of religion as understood by induction is only the result of development,

whereas it should be the prototype, the model which traces
the way of development. (1995, 2)

Here, Cohen argues that history ought not to determine the concept
of reason. On the contrary, it is reason that that is prior to and that
gives meaning to historical understanding. Cohen seeks to recover the
importance of philosophy, or at least ethics, in the face of history's
obsession with detail and reduction. The historical record, in other
words, potentially threatens Judaism's essence—ethics—portrayed by
Cohen here and others in his wake as the Jewish "contribution" to
Western civilization.

Cohen's student, Franz Rosenzweig (1886–1929), while disagree-
ing with his former teacher that ethics was the defining feature of
Judaism, nonetheless sought to remove the tradition from historical
study. For Rosenzweig, the Jewish people exist outside of history and,
thus, are immune to historical analysis and, because of this, are unique
(Hughes 2010a, 28–30; forthcoming). In part 3, book 1 of his *The Star
of Redemption*, Rosenzweig discusses three concepts in particular that
distinguish the Jewish people from all other nations: land, language,
and law. Language, he claims, is—like land and law—something
that, for most, is not eternal, but that which lives insofar as people
speak it. Language, then, has a unifying factor that connects a living
people to a specific land. Not so with Hebrew, however: "The eternal
people [as he likes to call the Jews] lost its own language and everywhere speaks the language of its external destinies, the language of
the people with whom it perchance dwells as a guest" (Rosenzweig
2005, 320). Whereas language traditionally locates a people in time,
the language of Israel removes itself, and by extension Israel, from
time and relocates it in eternity.

The privileged sphere of the Jewish people, according to Rosenzweig's reading, makes them a people apart. He sets them up as the
antithesis or counterpoint of the other nations. Because of this they
cannot be classified, understood, or analyzed using the methods used
for other peoples. And while one may argue that I am here collapsing
Rosenzweig's fascinating philosophical arguments into a set of historical claims, it would seem that this is indeed the logical conclusion of
his sentiments. The result is that Rosenzweig, like his teacher Cohen,
and unlike the majority of individuals discussed earlier in this chapter,
rejects historical analysis as too reductive and too simplistic to capture
the genius of the Jewish people.

This tension—between those who believe that Jews and Judaism
should be subject to social and historical analysis and those who do
not—takes us to the heart of this book's argument. We witness one

possible conclusion, whether logical or not, of Rosenzweig's argument in Heilman's claim that non-Jews cannot be the public face of Jewish studies programs because they do not embody "what it means to take Jewish life and culture seriously."

Gershom Scholem: The Reaction against Wissenschaft

Highly critical of the dialectic of history and ahistory witnessed in this chapter stands the towering figure of Gershom Scholem (1897–1982). Scholem was a German-born Israeli philosopher and historian. He is widely acknowledged as the founder of the modern, academic study of kabbalah (Jewish mysticism), developing its basic structural outlines and articulating its major themes at a time when the majority of Wissenchaft scholars surveyed above paid no attention to its study and largely wrote it off as irrational and obscurantist.[7] Appointed as the first professor of Jewish mysticism at the newly created Hebrew University of Jerusalem, Scholem began what would amount to a lifetime of collecting and cataloging the hundreds of kabbalistic manuscripts that few had interest in and that even fewer could decipher. In addition, Scholem was responsible for training three generations of scholars of Jewish mysticism (see Idel 1999, 91–114).

Although space does not permit a full-scale analysis of the writings of Gershom Scholem here, it is worth noting that his "corrective" to Wissenshaft des Judentums is, on some levels, no less ideologically charged. Whereas the likes of Zunz, Graetz, and Geiger had created an apologetical account of Judaism, one that marginalized the mystical as having no place at Judaism's rational core and one that was in sync with European modalities of modernity, Scholem would come to excoriate against this approach as too assimilationist and as too pathological. Instead, he argued that mysticism formed the vibrant core and hidden life that had sustained Judaism throughout its long history. It was this mystical impulse, moreover, that had a profound impact on Jewish history because, while often suppressed, it would surface when certain conditions arose and be responsible for powering change.[8] As a result, he set up his construction of Judaism in direct opposition to the earlier tradition of the academic study of Judaism. Like the scholars against whom he railed, he supported the idea of a rationalist study of Judaism (Biale 1982, 38–44); unlike them, however, the new rationalist science had to be grounded in the irrational or, as Biale suggests, "a rational account of the history of irrationalism" (Biale 1982, 38). Scholem sets as his goal the task of rebuilding "the entire structure of knowledge in terms of the historical experience of the Jew who lives among his own people and has no other accounts to make than the perception of the problems, the events and the thoughts according to their true being, in the framework of their historical function within the people" (Scholem 1997, 66). For Scholem, critical historical scholarship was both a means to understand the past and to reconstruct the present. In this respect, he was also highly critical of Jewish philosophers such as Hermann Cohen, Franz Rosenzweig, and Martin Buber, who had become very popular in the middle of the twentieth century. Scholem rejected both grand schemes in favor of careful historical analysis of the regnant literary sources of Judaism (see Magid 2008). He used history and philology to develop a legitimate Jewish theology in a world that could no longer support authentic mysticism. The kabbalah, under his careful and expert hand, became the perfect locus to counter the exaggerated rationalism of his predecessors; however, phenomenologically, Scholem's project was not unlike theirs. For him, esoteric movements were the motivating force of history, which offered renewal in the face of decay and calcification. Scholem offered his past, in other words, as the antidote to the rational past of his predecessors. It was a past, however, that, like theirs, represented an authenticity lacking in the present.

Conclusions

The aim of this chapter was to try to provide a general overview of the origins of the modern academic study of Judaism. Central to this origin was the uses and abuses of the historical record. How, for example, could history be applied to Jewish sources? And how could the great diversity of Jewish texts, from various times and places, be put within a comprehensive historical framework? These were among the central aims of those scholars who sought to make sense of Judaism and its sources independent of the ahistorical dimension of traditional, rabbinic Judaism and the supersessionist arguments supplied by christocentric European scholarship. Prevented from holding positions at German universities on account of their religion, this first generation of secularly trained Jewish scholars sought to develop a new academic program for Judaism. It is at this point that we can begin to speak of the beginnings of encountering Judaism academically.

Their enterprise, however, was fraught with tensions and was in direct response to a host of nonintellectual issues, almost all of which revolved around issues of making Jews "normal." The academic study of Judaism, in other words, was born from and developed as a response to issues of legal and social emancipation. Directed toward other Jews, these scholars felt the need to use scholarship as a way to educate them, to make them modern. Directed toward their detractors, they tried to show that Jews, like any other European nation state, also possessed their own history. The desire to articulate this history—to imagine it, to ascertain what drove it, and to reproduce it rhetorically—was predicated on a set of essentialist characteristics. This ultimately led to the conflation of scholarship, identity, and authenticity.

This chapter surveyed three distinct approaches to Jewish studies. The first witnessed the desire to historicize Judaism by showing its rational core, something that was believed to be responsible for generating the tradition's most important cultural and intellectual representations. These representations, according to the scholars examined above, stood for some of the most important achievements in all of Western civilization. The desire to historicize Judaism, however, quickly met with a concomitant approach to dehistoricize it. This approach sought to retain the "unique" elements of Jewishness by redefining it in terms of, for example, ethical monotheism (in the case of Hermann Cohen) or its ability to exist outside the normal parameters of other nation states (in the case of Franz Rosenzweig). We, then, witnessed a third approach to the study of Judaism—that of Gershom Scholem. His approach sought to take the historical and philological approach of the earliest generation of scholars, but use it to articulate a particular feature that he felt they had overlooked, the mystical and the esoteric. Rather that make Judaism rational, Scholem sought to show the tradition at its most irrational, something he felt defined the essence of Judaism and that made it distinct from other religious traditions.

All three of these approaches, thus, have distinct nationalist agendas that drive them. All were based, for example, on discovering some sort of essential characteristic or characteristics. Very few were interested in showing the rich counterpoints between Jews and non-Jews and the various ways in which the line between Jew/non-Jew blurs distinctions and is, in many ways, an artificial construction imposed by subsequent generations. But it probably could not have been otherwise. Zunz, Graetz, Geiger, and others were living at a time of crisis, trying to carve out a place for Jews in the face of a rising tide of anti-Semitism. Scholem, writing from the British mandate in Palestine and subsequently in the new State of Israel, was trying to establish a national homeland for Jews in the middle of an extremely traumatic century.

Within this context, Jews were "Other" and wrote their history as such. A more normalized approach to Jewish scholarship would have to wait for another time and another place.

3

Imagining Judaism

Scholar, Community, Identity

As witnessed in the previous chapter, scholars associated with Wissenschaft des Judentums saw it as their primary mandate to educate both Jews and non-Jews. They did this by demonstrating that Judaism possessed an essence, something that was both tangible and retrievable in the tradition's rich historical and textual tradition. The great paradox, of course, was that this was a tradition that these scholars had largely manufactured and interpreted in their own rationalist images. The major goal of their intellectual efforts was twofold. First, they desired to make Judaism intellectually respectable to non-Jews, something that would ideally lead to political emancipation for Jews. Second, if Jews could be shown to have a history, so the thinking went, they could then become productive members of society. And while they largely succeeded in the short term (by the late nineteenth century, Jews had received ostensible legal equality), the tragic fate of German (and other European) Jews in the midtwentieth century is both well known and well documented.[1]

From the very beginning, then, there has existed an intimate nexus between scholars of Judaism and the larger community of which they are a part. This is certainly not to claim that every scholar must necessarily be an apologist for Judaism, but it is to underscore the fact that there are real historical reasons as to why the majority of scholars of Judaism have traditionally been Jewish and why there has been a tendency to reify something amorphously referred to as "*the* Jewish experience." Yet, even though there have been significant reasons for why this has been the case in the past, my point—and this is what will be the subject matter of the concluding chapter—is that this no longer need be the case. Jewish studies has become such an integral part of both the religious studies and humanities curriculum that it need no longer be primarily entangled in the business of community and/or identity maintenance.

As scholars of Judaism migrated out of Europe, they took the assumptions of Wissenschaft with them. In Palestine[2] and America, scholarship on Jewish topics was to undergo major transformations. Despite these transformations, however, the legacy of the philological and historical approach would remain. The scholar of Judaism's relationship to community also began to undergo transformation. Whereas in Germany, the scholar of Judaism had articulated the political desires of larger European Jewish communities, in Israel and America the Jewish community saw itself reflected in the scholar of Judaism, who was now expected to uphold Jewish values and concerns. Framed somewhat more theoretically: in Germany, the scholar spoke for the community, and in America (and, to a lesser extent, Israel), the community spoke through the scholar. Perhaps it could even be said that in Germany scholars had expectations that were too high for their community, whereas in America, the situation was the opposite: communities had expectations that were too high concerning what Jewish studies was and what those scholars who engaged in it could realistically achieve. The relationship between scholar and community, in all of its many manifestations, forms one of the central features around which the academic study of Judaism revolves.

It is also worth noting that the migration out of Europe to Israel and America coincided with a change in scholarly language: from German to Hebrew in Israel, and from German to English in America. Such changes necessarily created a different set of political and ontological emphases. In Israel, scholars of Judaism saw themselves as intimately involved in the re/creation of a Jewish national culture and homeland. This Zionist impulse put a renewed interest in the texts of the Jewish past, but it was an interest that was not confined to the traditional, rabbinic model of interpretation. Although it was, in many ways, a continuation of the German model of philological and historical study, it was now undertaken in the traditional and "authentic" language of "the Jewish people."[3] In America, by contrast, community needs were somewhat different. There, the creation of positions in Semitics, the precursor to Jewish studies, offered a potential path toward social, cultural, and political inclusion.

The present chapter examines the movement of the academic study of Judaism out of Europe, eastward to Israel and westward to America, with the greatest emphasis on the latter. The goal, once again, is to show how Jewish studies scholarship is not simply an academic discipline, but intimately intertwined with a host of other features, virtually all of which revolve around the issue of something imagined and reified as Jewish peoplehood.

Scholars or Apologists?

In the previous chapter we witnessed how the academic study of Judaism was intimately connected to apologetics. If other nations possessed a national history, so the claim went, then Jews must also do so. In this respect, Jews were no different from other Europeans: a past was imagined and subsequently constructed to be magnificent—one in which all infelicities were neatly excised—that would in turn provide the seeds for contemporary renewal and the creation of a future. This was intimately connected to the rise of the modern university and the programmatic creation of all of the modern humanities and social sciences to make this past accessible (see, for example, Marchand 2009, xxi–xxix). So, although *certain* Jews now began to apply historical methods to the Jewish past, their aim—despite claims to the contrary—was not an "objective" recreation, but an attempt to improve fellow Jews in preparation for political emancipation.

Many associated with Wissenschaft des Judentums sought to clear an authoritative space for themselves outside of traditional institutions, such as the yeshiva and the synagogue. This hoped-for institutional space would have provided these Jews with a position to apply objective and nontraditional methods to the Jewish past, in much the same way that this was being done to the Christian past in various Protestant theological faculties. However, when Leopold Zunz approached the University of Berlin in 1848 with a well-thought-out proposal for creating a Chair in Jewish History and Literature, the faculty responded that they were not in the business of training rabbis (Schorsch 1994, 352).

The faculty's confusion of purpose, and its inability (or unwillingness) to understand Zunz's proposal, is one that reverberates into the present. Is it the goal of Jewish studies to train those engaged in apologetics or to produce critical scholars? Does the academic study of Judaism produce caretakers or critics? Certainly different constituencies have different views on such matters. A wealthy individual funding a chair of Jewish studies might have a radically different idea of what it means to study Judaism than the faculty member hired to fill the position. Although these issues will be addressed in more detail in a subsequent chapter, suffice it to mention here that, like those who received Zunz's initial proposal, many (including scholars and administrators, benefactors and detractors, Jews and non-Jews) are either not clear or do not want to be clear on the academic mission of Jewish studies within the university.

Despite calls for the creation of university posts in Jewish studies in Zunz's day, they never materialized. And this certainly had consequences for the subsequent development of the field. Because the state refused to fund such positions and because German institutions of higher learning refused to create posts to study Judaism, its academic study became dependent upon private benefactors and was largely carried out in seminaries. This meant that the scholarly study of Judaism, from its outset, developed outside of the university system. In the words of Suzanne L. Marchand, "during critical decades in the evolution of Orientalism and of German liberalism, those who were best suited to make the case for Judaism's cultural impact and scholarly traditions beyond the Old Testament were relegated to a sphere most Christian academics considered unscientific and exclusively parochial" (2009, 115). Christian Wiese argues that the rejection of Zunz's request was even more politically motivated, for to create a chair in Jewish studies would be tantamount to a "public acknowledgement of the equality of Judaism" and that this might counteract assimilation, "which was intended to be a gradual abandonment of Jewish identity" (2005, 82).

One of the most important repercussions of this dialectic meant that the academic study of Judaism was left to develop in religious and quasireligious seminaries, many of which were associated with the new denominations of Judaism (e.g., Reform, Conservative) that were just beginning to emerge. Moreover, as the previous chapter demonstrated, historical scholarship was used in the service of these denominational movements, and many of the earliest scholars of Judaism made their livelihoods as rabbis in these new, often more liberal-minded, movements because academic positions at German universities were closed to them. In 1840, for example, Leopold Zunz was appointed director of the Berlin Jewish Teachers' Seminary; and Abraham Geiger was the community rabbi in, among other places, Wiesbaden. The subsequent generation witnessed the foundation of even more seminaries associated with these versions of Judaism, such as the Jüdisch-Theologisches Seminar Fraenckel'scher Stiftung in Breslau (1854), the Hochschule für die Wissenschaft des Judentums in Berlin (1872), and the Rabbiner-Seminar in Berlin (1873).

The academic study of Judaism was intimately connected to the partisan politics associated with the Jewish community and its self-understanding. Each one of the institutions mentioned at the end of the previous paragraph sought to articulate a distinct version of Judaism that was believed to be in accord with the tenets of the modern world and, thus, of modern scientific advancements, of which history and philology ranked highly.

The study of Judaism in the non-Jewish German academy, in contrast, was only important when it was reduced solely to the Old Testament. This meant that much intellectual energy on the part of Jewish scholars of Judaism went into apologetical and emancipatory concerns (Wiese 2005, 81), the major focus of which was an examination of the period after the canonization of the Bible. This academic study of postbiblical Judaism, from its very inception, was not simply a scholarly enterprise. It sought, on the contrary, to dispel German prejudices against Jews and Judaism in order to legitimate both the religion and its practitioners in their eyes, and to make the case for political and legal emancipation. This meant showing the contributions that Jews and Judaism had made, among other things, to monotheism, to ethics, and to making the case that Judaism functioned as the bedrock from which the other monotheisms would eventually spring.

A Tale of Two Academies

The present section charts, in brief, the movement of Wissenschaft des Judentums from Germany to the formation of new academic centers in both Israel and America. Although there were manifold reasons for this migration to new shores—the rise of Zionism, increased European anti-Semitism, the world wars, which culminated in the Holocaust, the formation of the State of Israel in 1948—my focus here is on how Jewish studies is intertwined with these larger events and how the latter have contributed to the various ways that Judaism has been encountered, both academically and intellectually, in the middle and late twentieth century.

If Wissenschaft des Judentums was largely concerned with emancipation within Europe, there simultaneously arose in subsequent generations those who were increasingly critical of its failure. Perhaps nowhere is this critique on display more clearly than in Scholem's examination discussed in the previous chapter. Scholars such as Scholem sought, in direct opposition to earlier scholars, to develop a model of Jewish studies that could aid in the creation of a Jewish national culture by reconnecting it to the historic roots of the Jewish people. This meant, as David Myers explains, "a 'return' to the

Hebrew language, and then through 'restoration' to the ancestral land of Israel" (1995, 25).

If scholars of Wissenschaft had written largely in German, the language in which many of the scholarly methods were developed, a new generation of scholars began to write in Hebrew. Whereas the former permitted a critical distance from the Jewish past (Myers 1995, 25), the latter was in conversation with this past and the religious texts that came out of it, using the modern language of Hebrew to articulate the ancient language of Hebrew. This change in language—a change back to a language that defined earlier eras of Hebraic activity—certainly had the potential to make the study of Judaism more insular. This is not to say that there was a huge rush on the part of non-Jewish German scholars to read works of Jewish history written by Jews in German, but now, as Jewish studies began to be written in Hebrew, this was no longer even theoretically possible. In this regard, the switch to Hebrew as a language of scholarship coincided with a turn inward. As Scholem himself is once said to have remarked, "it is difficult for the writer of Hebrew ever to silence the powerful echoes of the divine faith and messianic expectation that permeate the ancient language" (qtd. in Myers 1995, 25).

The name given to this Hebrew enterprise was "*hokhmot Yisrael*," perhaps best translated as "The Wisdom of Israel," a term that resonates with a reverence for the tradition and its sources. This Hebrew notion of *hokhmah* is certainly a far cry form the Germanic notion of "science" (*Wissenschaft*). Although space does not permit me to examine the various individuals and movements associated with it,[4] suffice it to say that this model of scholarship—one of, for the most part, reverence—became a cornerstone of the new Institute of Jewish Studies, which was to form the core or heart of the newly formed Hebrew University in Jerusalem in 1924. Many regarded this institute of higher Jewish learning as part of an essential nationalist mission to build a Jewish homeland in Palestine. In the words of Judah L. Magnes, the first president of the Hebrew University, "Since the highest aim of the Institute must be scientific investigation, this means that we do not want our Institute to be like a provincial faculty or to make it a factory for exams and doctoral degrees. Our desire is that the Institute stand on a *scientific* plateau that is permeated throughout with [the ethos] of science, and whose goal is the revival of Jewish science" (qtd. in Myers 1995, 56). Magnes' lofty goals, including the revival of a "Jewish science," would prove hard to articulate and to achieve. What, for example, is a "Jewish science"—of what do its first principles consist, and how are they deployed? The Jewish population of Palestine nearly doubled in the following years requiring a university curriculum to educate its new inhabitants. As Hitler came to power in Germany, an influx of Jews—including German Jewish scholars—made their way to Palestine. The movement of a group of scholars from Europe to Palestine, however, seems to have prevented the type of model that both Scholem and Magnes desired. The European training of these first scholars of Jewish studies at the newly created Hebrew University of Jerusalem made them the direct heirs of their German Jewish forbearers. And although some, like Scholem, sought to create a new paradigm in Jewish scholarship, the results were certainly mixed from a historiographical point of view. Proclaimed as liberators of the new academic study of Judaism, concludes Myers, "they must also be seen, in part, as continuators of the institutional and intellectual heritage of Wissenschaft des Judentums" (Myers 1995, 177).

Let me focus solely on my own area of research—medieval Jewish philosophy—as a brief case study of some of the tensions and fractures of the study of Judaism in Israel. Shortly after its formation, the faculty of the institute and the board of governors of the university sought to appoint someone to fill a newly created chair in medieval Jewish philosophy. It is interesting to note that this chair was not to be appointed into the philosophy department in the broader humanities faculty, but in the Institute of Jewish Studies. The study of medieval Jewish philosophy—or Jewish philosophy more generally conceived—was conceptualized as both separate and distinct from non-Jewish philosophy. "Jewish" philosophy, in other words, unlike "general" philosophy, was by its subject matter (i.e., philosophy as done by "Jews" as opposed to "Gentiles") regarded as somehow unique. The implication here is that to appreciate truly Jewish philosophy, it must be kept apart from "secular" philosophy and studied according to its own inner rhythm or dynamics. To this day, those seeking to engage in the study of Jewish philosophy take such courses in the Department of Jewish Thought (*Makhshevet Yisrael*)—one of the departments within the Institute of Jewish Studies—as opposed to the Department of Philosophy (*philosophia*), wherein non-Jewish philosophy (from Plato to Derrida) is taught.

This, of course, creates a set of problems. For one thing, Jewish philosophy and Judaism more generally are studied in isolation from other cultures and, by extension, the critical tools developed to study these other cultures. There is the implication that Jewish data—or, at least data that is constructed as "Jewish"—need not conform to established disciplinary norms and structures. Second, this creates a huge double standard: what is Jewish can be studied one way, and the larger cultural contexts in which Jewish texts were produced are approached in an entirely different way. This further leads to the reification of what is "Jewish" and what is "non-Jewish." Third, it perpetuates the German Wissenschaft model where Judaism was kept separate from the "normal" university curriculum. This risks further contributing to the seminary model wherein the academic study of Judaism began decades earlier. Fourth, it implies that there is something inherently special or unique about Jewish data, to such an extent that it demands to be articulated in its own departments and presumably using its own methods.

This model is still alive and well in Israel. Time and again I have heard that the only place to study medieval Jewish philosophy is in Israel, whether at the Hebrew University of Jerusalem or in one of the other universities that have sprung up over the years (e.g., Ben Gurion University of the Negev in Beersheba, Bar Ilan University in Ramat Gan, Tel Aviv University, University of Haifa). The Zionist impulse guiding this implies that a vibrant intellectual culture on matters Judaica is not possible outside of the land of Israel. This tension between Israeli scholarship and that produced in the diaspora, particularly America, is one that remains to this day.

Because this study is primarily focused on how Judaism is situated within the American academy, the remainder of this chapter will examine the rise and eventual florescence of Jewish studies on American campuses.

Jewish Studies in America

Much like their German Jewish counterparts, American Jews also regarded university recognition as the pathway to achieve social and cultural inclusion (Ritterband and Wechsler 1994, 10).[5] Once again, then, university campuses and the academic study of Jewish topics became one of the primary institutional spaces for Jewish normalization. By the late nineteenth century, sixteen Jews occupied academic positions in various university Semitics departments, where Jewish studies would largely be taught until after the middle of the twentieth century. The teaching of Jewish subjects within American universities, as many influential Jews hoped, was to establish "university-based Jewish learning that could serve both a parent discipline and the Jewish community" (Ritterband and Wechsler 1994, 10), a delicate balance that the discipline has still largely tried to maintain to this day.

Many of these positions in Jewish Semitics, however, were in Old Testament and biblical Hebrew grammar, something that was largely in keeping with America's emphasis on biblical religion. Positions in Jewish Semitics appeared in universities with significant Jewish communities and were largely based on community support: University of California, University of Chicago, Columbia, Harvard, Johns Hopkins, and the University of Pennsylvania. Even in these early years, write Ritterband and Wechsler, university "presidents expected that successful Semitics programs would encourage the munificence of the local Jewish community for other projects" (1994, 23). The goal of creating largely privately funded positions in Jewish topics was related to encouraging even larger financial commitments for all sorts of other non-Jewish activities and programs from wealthy Jewish donors. At a time when Jewish community building was beginning in earnest, perceived access to numerous American cultural institutions, such as the university, were now within reach in ways that they never were in Europe.

University recognition of Jewish Semitics in turn created a sense of social, religious, and intellectual acceptance on the part of many within the Jewish community. Although not as involved in the sectarian debates as it had been in Europe, Jewish scholarship tended to be supported primarily by Reform Jews, many of whom sought both to legitimate and to strengthen themselves in the face of more traditional denominations. Many of the latter were either not interested in or were outwardly hostile to the higher criticism of university Semitics. By the end of the nineteenth century, Jewish Semitics in these select institutions thrived, largely owing to "American Jewish communal subventions" (Ritterband and Wechsler 1994, 35). Increasingly, however, such communal support began to diminish for a number of reasons. Some were certainly economic and sociological, but also important was the fact that numerous Jewish scholars of Jewish data no longer knew how to speak to communities, seeking instead professional as opposed to community recognition.

This tension between academy and community, professional obligations and communal ones, was present at the outset of Jewish scholarship in America. As scholars interested in professional fame produced highly technical studies on obscure areas of study, the community became less interested in supporting such study. Despite these tensions and the repercussions in the twentieth century, this initial community support for Jewish Semitics created an academic foothold for Jewish studies scholarship.

A good early example of the plight of Jewish Semitics in America may be found in Felix Adler (1851–1933), the son of one of the leading figures of Reform Judaism in America, Samuel Adler, rabbi of Temple Emanu-El in New York City. In 1874, after it had become clear that the young Felix would not follow his father's footsteps into the rabbinate, members of his father's congregation funded a professorship in Hebrew and Oriental literature at Cornell University and nominated Adler for the position. Writing of the appointment in the same year, the *Jewish Messenger*, a weekly periodical that was published out of New York City, proclaimed,

> It is significant of the progress of culture in this country, when a thriving education institution—such as Cornell University—adds to its faculty a young and talented Israelite to fill the professorship of Hebrew and Oriental Literature . . . We hail the appointment of a Hebrew professor as a grand concession to the liberality of the age, and congratulate the faculty of Cornell University in having thus demonstrated their freedom from prejudice . . . [Adler's supporters who financed the position] have the satisfaction of having not only placed their friend-protégé in an honorable position, *but elevated the Jewish name and Jewish interests in the opinion of the world, again demonstrating that the Jew has higher ideas than mere moneymaking.* (qtd. in Ritterband and Wechsler 1994, 47; my italics)

In this passage we see how Adler's religious and ethnic identity means as much to the editors of the *Jewish Messenger* as his scholarly potential or capabilities. Although Adler's position would eventually not be renewed, and his vision of Judaism would eventually alienate many of his initial supporters, this quotation reveals just how important it was that these positions in Jewish subjects be held by individuals who embody a positive Jewish identity, whatever that may consist of or whatever the community perceived it to consist of.

As long as the academic study of Judaism remained within Semitics, this study risked being little more than a subdiscipline of Semitic linguistics. Confined to the study of the Bible, the study of Judaism reinforced earlier stereotypes that Jewish history ended as Christianity's began. This coincided with restrictions on Jewish enrollments at many American universities, and other hostilities (Norwood 2009, 1–25). Positions to study Judaism remained largely funded by Jewish philanthropists, and this created all sorts of potential problems, ones that persist to this day. Was, for example, the *academic* study of Judaism being included in university curricula solely because wealthy Jewish benefactors were underwriting its cost? Were they being indulged so that they would give even larger gifts to the university? If universities were truly interested in the academic study of Judaism, why did they not contribute any resources to its study and instead wait for private monies? What happens if those who occupy such endowed chairs are critical of causes in which the community or the donor believes?

These questions are, of course, as relevant today as they were in the early nineteenth century. Institutional anti-Semitism, then as now, means that benefactors do not always want to fund disinterested scholarship. The subsequent decline of Jewish Semitics in the interwar periods saw a concomitant rise in and communal support for Jewish seminaries, such as Hebrew Union College in Cincinnati, Dropsie College in Philadelphia, Yeshiva College in New York, and the Chicago College of Jewish Studies (now known as the Spertus Institute). For many, these institutions offered a better venue for teaching and learning about Jewish topics. In 1903, for example, Solomon Schechter, himself associated with the Jewish Theological Seminary in New York, which was responsible for the training of rabbis in the Conservative movement, wrote that these seminaries were places where "Rabbis [could] begin to write books which were till now the exclusive monopoly of University Professors" (qtd. in Ritterband and Wechsler 1994, 141).

This tension between the study of Judaism in university and seminary settings was—and, indeed, still is—reflected in how Jewish data was connected to larger academic currents. Many seminaries were not just need-based alternatives to the exclusion of Jewish topics (and Jews) at universities, but also places where new generations of rabbis were trained. However, critics of such seminaries argued that they were not places where disinterested and objective scholarship took place, something that could only be done within a university setting.

Post–World War II Developments

The 1960s witnessed the formation of independent Jewish studies programs and even departments in colleges and universities across the United States (for more background see the studies in Blumenthal 1976; Greenspahn 2000; Bush 2011, 57–66). This coincided with the rise of ethnic studies and the desire to include groups traditionally excluded from the canons of scholarship (e.g., African Americans, American Indians, women). The emphasis was less on the supposed universalism of previous generations and more on the particular claims of identity of the occluded (Szanton 2004, 1–15). In terms of Jewish studies, this also coincided with a renewed sense of pride marked by Israeli victory in the Six Day War of 1967.

Jewish studies departments, then, could function as definers of identity for Jewish students on campus, as places that celebrated Jewish contributions to Western civilization, and as a sign that Jewish topics had finally arrived on American campuses. Yet, this connection between identity and scholarship is, as we have seen throughout this study, always a problematic one. It assumes, for example, that identity is fixed and stable, and that Jewish studies is in the business of teaching about Jewish identity as opposed to showing how it is just as constructed as any other identity formation. Since the 1960s, when the study of Judaism had become increasingly entangled with area/ethnic studies and given Israel's victories in the Middle East, Jewish studies took a tremendous turn inward.

Relatedly, the 1960s also witnessed the rise of the secular study of religion at state universities. Although still exhibiting a Protestant bias (see Orsi 2005, 185–89), there was nevertheless a desire to study and present other religions of the globe to American undergraduates. This presentation, however, was not without its own categorical biases (see, for example, Masuzawa 2005; McCutcheon 1997). Judaism, thus, became "a permanent subdivision of the study of religion" (Ritterband and Wechsler 1994, 197), and it was in such departments that it was largely conceptualized and taught. Whereas some relished the thought of studying and comparing Judaism to other religions—what we can call the universalist vision—others believed that a disinterested approach to Judaism was out of sync with traditional norms: "For university teachers of Judaica to fail to inculcate in their students the notion of study as a mitzvah [i.e., commandment] is to be as unfaithful to their discipline as for teachers of physics to fail to inculcate an acceptance of the scientific method" (Levy 1974, 15). This tension is certainly not unique to the academic study of Judaism within departments of religious studies. It is, however, worth noting in this regard that the model of scholarship preferred in departments of religious studies does tend to gravitate toward the ecumenical and the interfaith, thereby making the study of Judaism in such departments—much like the study of other religions—overly apologetical (see, e.g., McCutcheon 1997). Although, it is certainly worth noting that many who were uncomfortable with the largely Protestant presuppositions endemic to religious studies made the case that Judaism should be studied in departments of Jewish studies. However, this leads to the concomitant fear that connections to larger established disciplines might be muted or severed, meaning that some might think that there is some unique "Jewish way" to study Jewish data.

Finding Institutional Space

Writing in 1966, Arnold Band, then a young professor of Hebrew literature at UCLA, noted "a spread of Jewish studies as an accepted academic discipline in the American liberal-arts colleges and universities" (Band 1966, 3). Reflecting the growth of positions across American campuses, there arose a new generation of young scholars who sought to communicate with one another on an academic level. In response, Leon Jick decided to organize a colloquium at his home institution, Brandeis University in Waltham, Massachusetts from September 7 to September 10, 1969. With financial support from the Boston philanthropist Philip W. Lown, Jick convened a group of forty-seven scholars with the intention of discussing their work and addressing problems in the new field of Jewish studies (Jick 1970, 1–3). Shortly thereafter, the Association for Jewish Studies (AJS), to this day the major organization for scholars of Judaica, was founded. This new organization quickly replaced the earlier American Academy of Jewish Research (AAJR), which had been founded in 1919. The major goals of this latter Academy were "the organization of periodic meetings for the presentation of learned papers; the publication of scholarly work in Judaica; and the promotion of fellowship and cooperation between scholars and learned societies in America and other countries."[6] By the mid-1960s, as Kristen Loveland well notes, "younger scholars saw the AAJR as an exclusive organization dominated by elder statesmen unable to meet the transforming field's need" (Loveland 2008, 3). Whereas one had to be elected into the AAJR, the new organization was open to all working in the field of Jewish studies.

In his contribution to the proceedings, Joseph L. Blau wrote that the task of this newly formed, if rather inchoate, discipline of Jewish studies was to create "a place in American higher education for the studies in the life, thought, and culture of Jews, past and present, not only as a means of stimulating the enrichment of educational content now, and as a factor in Jewish survival in time to come, but also because we are convinced that these studies have an intrinsic value that is like and yet unlike comparable studies of other ethnic groups" (Blau 1970, 90). This idea that the study of Jews and Judaism is both "like and yet unlike" the study of other ethnic groups returns us to the heart of the academic study of Judaism. What does it mean to be both "like and unlike" other groups, religions, or cultures? This is surely the claim that every area or ethnic studies program makes of its particular subject matter. If Jews and Judaism are like other groups they can presumably be understood using the same methods used to analyze those other groups. If, however, they are "unlike" them, this means that Jews are somehow sui generis and accordingly must be understood on their own terms, something that amounts to little more than a quasireligious or theological claim. Jewish studies, according to this rationale, straddles the universal and the particular, the repeatable and the unique. Also significant is Blau's comment that the academic study of Judaism should be concerned with "Jewish survival." Again, then, we witness the intersection of the scholarly study of Judaism and how it is intimately bound up with the fate of Jewish communities. It is perhaps worth noting that at this initial meeting of scholars of Jewish studies, only Jewish practitioners of Jewish studies were invited to discuss the future of the field (Loveland 2008, 3), a decision that one participant acknowledged served as "recognition that more is at stake in Jewish Studies than increasing research and teaching efforts in the field" (Greenberg 1970, 116). The fact that non-Jewish scholars of Jewish studies were not invited might not be as odd as it first appears when it is remembered that, at the time, there were very few non-Jewish scholars of Jewish studies. Moreover, because there were very few places where scholars of Judaica could be trained in these early years outside of Columbia (where Salo Wittmayer Baron taught), Harvard (Harry A. Wolfson), and Brandeis (Alexander Altmann), the majority of scholars arrived at Jewish studies through rabbinical training (Loveland 2008, 3).

Perhaps indicative of the fact that the overwhelming majority of Jewish studies scholars were Jewish, the earliest AJS conferences distributed *benchers* (small prayer books) with the AJS logo, courtesy of Ktav Publishing House. In addition, the *birkhat ha-mazon* (Grace after Meals) was recited at communal dinners (Loveland 2008, 7). And, as Loveland writes, although some AJS members expressed discomfort with the appearance of public religiosity at an academic conference, many argued for the continuation of the communal ritual (2008, 7).[7]

The need for scholarly legitimation, on the one hand, and the acknowledgment of the uniqueness of the Jewish tradition, on the other, is one of the tensions that runs throughout the academic study of Judaism. An excellent example of some tensions facing the young organization may be witnessed in the debate between Harvey

Branscomb and Samuel Sandmel concerning the nature of community involvement.[8] Branscomb, the Chancellor Emeritus at Vanderbilt
University, explained his involvement in creating endowed chairs in
Jewish studies "in what might have been called at the time two WASP
universities" (Branscomb 1970, 95). He goes on to explain the criteria
for the person to be hired in such positions:

> In the first place, we had to find someone willing to take
> the job, willing to work, that is, in a not unfriendly but
> nevertheless alien religious environment. He must be inter-
> ested in the problem of communication across frontiers too
> often closed. He should be a person of outgoing tempera-
> ment who would enjoy contact with Christian scholars and
> invite friendship in turn. Without question he must be a
> good scholar. And finally, *he must be a loyal representative
> of his faith*. This last was based on the belief that to correct
> inveterate misunderstandings and prejudices *it was impor-
> tant to convey not only the literary and historical facts but also
> the ethos of the Jewish faith as well, its spiritual meaning to its
> adherents*. (1970, 97; my italics)

Branscomb was trying to create a position in Jewish studies in the
southern United States, at Duke University, in the 1940s. Responding
to Branscomb, Samuel Sandmel wrote an essay entitled "Scholar or
Apologist?" In this essay, he puts his finger on the paradoxical position facing chairs in Jewish studies: "Hoffman's lament[9] and Branscomb's wish for the incumbent to be a practicing Jew implies, at the
minimum, that the incumbent would be a Jewish spokesman in some
way. How can these two opinions be reconciled with the supposition
of the academic world that a scholar is, relatively, objective, dispas-
sionate, and—above all—committed to the impartial search for the
truth and not to some antecedent convictions? (Sandmel 1970, 104).
Sandmel here recognizes the problems associated with positions in
Jewish studies at American universities. Despite his awareness of the
problem—whether those who staff such positions should be first-rate
scholars or someone who is, to use Branscomb's words, "a loyal rep-
resentative of his faith"—he nevertheless acknowledges that chairs in
Jewish studies represent "the most important development in modern
American Judaism" (1970, 110). Although Sandmel began his essay
clearly stating the difference between a scholar and an apologist, by
the time he nears the end of his essay he is admittedly not nearly
as confident. "My thinking," he writes, "is the more clouded by my

resentment that the situation has arisen in which the dilemma exists, for I should have preferred that it had not arisen" (1970, 111). The "situation" of which he speaks is anti-Semitism, anti-Israel sentiments, and the rise of active and articulate Muslim student groups on campus. (Keep in mind he is writing, in 1969, only two years after the Six-Day War.) He ends his essay on a rather ominous note, one that is telling indeed for a particular strand of Jewish studies scholarship: "We, ourselves, when we can manage the situation, ought never be apologists in our persons; it is our scholarship which should be our apologetics" (1970, 111).

Scholar and Community

The relationship between a scholar of religion and the community that he studies is a problematic one even at the best of times. Is it the goal of the scholar to uphold the values that the people of a particular religious community hold dear, a community to which she has largely devoted her academic life, or, is it to go about her labor without due regard for communal sensibility? This tension is particularly acute in Jewish studies where not infrequently the scholar of Judaism holds a position that has been endowed by someone in the local community, someone moreover who, if still living, often has particular ideas about what Judaism is and what scholarship should communicate to others. This is certainly not to imply that the academic study of Judaism is either more or less apologetical than other religions. However, it is to make the point that the nature of the relationship between scholar and community is a complex one in general and in Jewish studies in particular.

Jewish communities, as we have seen in this chapter, have always played an important role in lobbying for and funding positions in Jewish studies. This is connected to the fact that such communities envisage the primary goal of Jewish studies as advocating for Jewish students and, not infrequently, a pro-Israel position on campus. Historically, this advocacy is certainly related to the fact that Jewish subjects initially entered the university curriculum on account of private bequests. Without such monies, then, there could not initially have been a study of Jewish topics. While the situation is certainly better today, the great diversity of Jewish studies programs and departments in the United States is in no small measure still based on such nonacademic munificence.[10] This has meant that, at least in America, Jewish studies from its inception has had tremendous community support. It should come as no surprise, then, that the rise and florescence of Jewish studies have been and continue to be directly proportionate to the support of the community.

Jewish communities, especially in America, have sought to create an institutional space into which they have emanated their desires for inclusion and acceptance. The scholar of Judaism, then, is frequently perceived as a metonym for Jewish community. The great paradox is that this perception exists among both community members and academic colleagues. Whereas the former neither understand nor are particularly interested in academic matters, the latter often regard the Jewish studies scholar as an apologist or advocate for things Jewish and the programs that such scholars inhabit as supported by private monies, whose primary aim is getting Jewish students interested in their religious tradition. One of the central issues that confronts the scholar of Jewish studies, one that has been around since its inception, revolves around that of advocacy. What is the perceived role of the Jewish studies scholar on campus? Are scholars of Judaism "caretakers" of the tradition or its "critics"? These two roles have radically different repercussions. The critic sees it as his or her role to interrogate all aspects of tradition (from concepts such as "chosenness" to the very construction and maintenance of something known as "Jewishness"), whereas the concern of the caretaker is maintaining the status quo, often using the nonscholarly language of reverence (see Lincoln 1996, 225–27). While these two roles are certainly not unique to the academic study of Judaism, they become particularly relevant when it is remembered that the overwhelming majority of Jewish studies scholars are themselves Jews. While I am interested neither in levels of religious observance (as, say Branscomb was) nor in specific relations with community, my concern is perception. How Jewish studies scholars perceive themselves and how others perceive them, both inside and outside the academy, are ultimately two sides of the same coin.

Although the answer will be deferred to a later chapter, it is certainly worth asking: What happens when private monies are used to fund the study of a particular religion (or particular religions) at a public university? What happens if a non-Jew is the best-qualified candidate for a position that has been endowed by the local Jewish community? Or, perhaps framed somewhat differently, what happens if an academic search committee finds a non-Jew to be the best possible candidate for a position in which the local benefactors either want or insist upon a Jew to fill the position? At a time when state funds are drying up, the creation of new, privately funded positions becomes increasingly attractive to administrators.[11] Again, the study of Judaism provides an important *exempli gratia*, both positive and negative, of the issues and stakes that are involved in the creation of such positions.

As we should come to expect, the role of community in the formation of Jewish studies is not a simple one that neatly reduces to a set of apologetics. The late nineteenth and early twentieth centuries were a time of anti-Semitic discrimination in America both inside and outside of the academy, and when universities taught matters of "religion" they did so largely from a Protestant perspective. Divinity schools trained young students for the ministry, and when and if they thought about Judaism, they largely did so from a supersessionist perspective (see Hughes 2010b). Hebrew was studied, but it was the Hebrew of the Old Testament and not the rabbinic or modern iterations of the language. To attempt to redress such oversights and to reveal something of the contributions of Jews to Western civilization wealthy benefactors sought to create positions in Jewish studies. And although "oversights" and "contributions" were frequently citied as reasons for funding, a major reason was—not unlike the reasons for the emergence of Wissenschaft in Germany—to show non-Jews that Jewish topics and subject matters belonged at universities, just as Jews belonged in American society.

In its early years, the community had much invested, both politically and financially, in positions that introduced Jewish data into academic curricula. This, it seems to me, goes a long way to explaining the fact that the overwhelming ethnic and religious background of those engaged in Jewish studies is Jewish. When non-Jews taught about Judaism, they tended to do so in a way that provided the background to the emergence of Christianity. If communities were to fund such positions, the last thing they wanted was to have Christians hired to maintain this status quo. Unlike today, these early years of the study of Judaism in America witnessed donors dictating who would be hired—sometimes qualified Jews, sometimes local rabbis. This issue once again returns us to the one raised by Heilman in chapter 1. Can non-Jews, repackaging his concerns, be expected to uphold Jewish community interests on campus? Does the lack of an ethnic or religious affiliation prevent scholars of Judaism from having sufficient empathy for their subject matter? At the same time, however, we should not assume that "Jewish" scholars of Jewish data are necessarily content with their perceived affiliation with community. Even though local benefactors may well fund their positions, many have frequently tried to distance themselves from the perception that they are simply the extension of the local community.[12]

Ontological legitimation and the demands of scholarship, however, are not the best of bedfellows. This is certainly not to make the claim that local communities control what Jewish studies scholars can and cannot say or publish. However, it is to state that, whether we like it or not, the academic study of Judaism in America has been and, for the most part, continues to be intimately connected to community concerns and vice versa. Community programming, fundraising at the local and national levels, and the general blurring of academic and nonacademic interaction are frequently the order of the day in most Jewish studies departments and/or programs. This has been exacerbated in recent years by the rise of wealthy funding agencies—such as the Tikvah and Posen Foundations—that have distinct ideological agendas that emerge from various political concerns (see chapter 5 in this text). If the community wants support for a particular issue on anti-Semitism (whether of the new, Middle Eastern variety or of the old, European variety) or to justify a particular stance (often pro-Zionistic) in the Middle East, the local scholar is often called upon. It is unfortunate that much community programming no longer involves adult education, but the legitimation of entrenched beliefs on a host of what are increasingly becoming well-worn subjects. Speaking in 1988, long after Jewish studies had made its way into the university curriculum, Lawrence Baron, director of the Jewish Studies Program at San Diego State University proclaimed after he had gotten community criticism for bringing a Christian scholar to speak about the Jewishness of Jesus, "I'm not sure universities always do their best to tell people up front that these are academic, not advocacy, programs" (Mahler 1994, 55).

Once again, we see clearly how the history or genealogy of the discipline dramatically affects its modern makeup. Jewish studies, although not infrequently funded by community monies, nevertheless does surprisingly well—for the most part—when it comes to checking the influence of these interests. However, the fact that virtually every endowed chair of Jewish studies in the United States is held by a Jew is certainly neither coincidental nor unproblematic.[13] I do not think that these overwhelming numbers can be reduced to the argument that non-Jews do not want to study Judaism. Anecdotally, the great majority of students in Jewish studies classes, especially outside of the northeast corridor, are non-Jewish. Why, as I asked in a previous chapter, do such students rarely go on to study Jewish data, outside of the Old Testament/Hebrew Bible, at the graduate level? The connections among community, scholarship, and ethnicity have become so entrenched in the academic study of Judaism that they need to be seriously rethought. It strikes me that the future of the field depends on it.

Once again, we witness the tension between the universal and the particular. How should Jewish data be taught? Universally, so that such data can function as but one *exempla gratia* of a larger set of humanistic concerns? Or particularly, in which case Jewish history, texts, and the like are considered sui generis? This tension between the universal and the particular, as we have seen, runs throughout both Jewish history and the academic study of Judaism. How, at least in the discipline of religious studies, ought Judaism to intersect with a larger set of theoretical and methodological concerns? Although one could make the case that this is true for every religious tradition that finds itself under the disciplinary canopy of religious studies, the history of how Judaism came to be studied academically within the American academy—its traditional exclusion and subsequent inclusion on account of community funding—provides a number of discursive sites for the academic study of religion more generally.

Conclusions

This chapter was a general overview of the rise of the academic study of Judaism in the years following its inception as Wissenschaft des Judentums in Germany. Using a basic historical narrative, I argued that the academic study of Jewish data in all of its iterations (Wissenschaft des Judentums, Hokhmot Yisrael, Jewish studies) has been intimately connected to the larger Jewish community. This is not necessarily a disinterested relationship, but one that has had significant repercussions on the many ways that Judaism has been funded and situated on campuses in North America and beyond. In the following chapter, I move to several case studies that will permit me to examine this in greater detail.

4

Take Ancient Judaism for Example

Five Case Studies

The previous chapter examined the complex relationship that has developed between Jewish studies and Jewish community, showing how the former over its long and convoluted history both mirrors and responds to the situation of the latter. The tensions inherent in this relationship are not simply of recent provenance, but have been there from the inception of Jewish studies in the early decades of the nineteenth century. In the American context, this relationship says as much about Jewish desire for inclusion as it does about university administrators' traditional unwillingness to include Jewish topics within academic curricula for their own sake. Such community support still largely sustains the academic study of Judaism and, despite the caveats raised in the previous chapter, has largely contributed to its present vitality.[1] However, such support also has the potential to undermine Jewish studies, especially when it is connected to particular ideological commitments. Recent years, for example, have witnessed the creation of numerous wealthy organizations (e.g., Schusterman Foundation,[2] Tikvah Fund,[3] Posen Foundation[4]) that are now in the business of subsidizing the academic study of Judaism. Although such support has its origins in the narrative told in the previous chapter, these organizations are now often connected to larger political projects, ones that have the potential to threaten the longterm viability of the field. Before examining this in greater detail, however, it is first necessary to return to the formative years of Jewish studies in America in order to try to tell the story (or, better, stories) of how Jewish data were integrated into the academic study of religion.

The primary place that Judaism is encountered academically within the university today is in departments of religious studies.[5] Therein, depending upon the scholar in question, Jewish data can either be opened up by or closed to the theoretical and comparative models supplied by this larger field of inquiry.[6] Whereas larger disciplines can and should be extremely useful in understanding the relationship between Jews and non-Jews, including the construction of Jewish identity (see, for example, Bodian 1999; D. Boyarin 2008; Hughes 2010a; Wolfson 2005, 2010), the particularist model that tends to reify Jews and Jewish data can still take precedence. There exist at least two potential problems in situating Judaism within departments of religious studies. Primary is the overwhelming propensity of the latter discipline toward theoretical models that stress ecumenicism and appreciation. Second and concomitantly, there is the desire on the part of many who study Judaism—as indeed there is with those working with data from other religious traditions—to avoid those paradigms within the larger discipline that are overly critical of traditional paradigms within the academic study of religion.

The academic study of religion—referred to in the past as the history of religions or comparative religion—was first introduced as a subsection within the American Oriental Society (AOS) in 1897.[7] In 1891, Columbia, Johns Hopkins, and the University of Pennsylvania founded the American Lectures on the History of Religions (ALHR) with the aim of encouraging "path-breaking scholarship through a lecture and book series."[8] As more and more colleges and universities began to offer courses on the history of religions in the late nineteenth and early twentieth centuries, Judaism could, at least in theory, now be studied in new intellectual contexts and using new methodological frameworks. However, as Ritterband and Wechsler do well to point out, Judaism's inclusion within this new and so-called "objective" curriculum was often precarious and was frequently contingent upon the answers to at least three relevant questions:

- Was the [history of religions to be] useful in the teaching of missionaries, or was it a "value free" academic discipline?

- What were the methodological criteria for introducing specific religions into the arena of research? Would scholars emphasize primitive or sophisticated religions?

- Would philologically trained Judaica scholars apply their skills to the study of Judaism [within the larger context supplied by the history of religions]? (Ritterband and Wechsler 1994, 190)

These questions are important and reveal the potentially tenuous position of the study of Judaism within the larger context of the study of religion in its earliest years in America. The first question, for example, revolves around how the field envisages the study of Judaism. Is Judaism an important component of the curriculum on its own terms, or is it included and studied as the means to provide the backdrop to the rise of Christianity? This supersessionist model, it should be recalled, has been around since the origins of Jewish studies as an academic subject in the early nineteenth century. Although certainly not as overt today, its modern incarnation is witnessed in the very structure of departments of religious studies, which tend to have numerous faculty members for the various temporal periods of Christianity (ancient, medieval, modern, American), but usually only one person to study all of Judaism, from the Bible to the modern State of Israel. Implicit in this disciplinary demographic is that Judaism is not a particularly complex religious form. In addition, it is not unusual to have this Jewish studies position staffed by a local rabbi, whether because such an individual is regarded as knowledgeable of things "Jewish" or more often than not, to cut costs because a full-time tenure line does not have to be created. The third question addresses the self-perception of the scholar of Judaism within such departments and vice versa. Do the larger theoretical and methodological concerns within departments of religious studies have any relevance for understanding Jewish texts? What relevance, for example, do theoretical concerns that were and indeed still are advanced by scholars working on "Eastern" or "non-monotheistic" data have for the so-called great texts of Judaism, such as the Mishnah and Talmuds? Although the answers to such questions, as Ritterband and Wechsler note, is determined by the particular department and the individual scholar in question, read on another level, such questions further exacerbate—as the present chapter will make clear—some of the tensions already inherent to the study of Judaism in particular and within the larger disciplinary parameters of religious studies in more general terms.

As witnessed in the introduction, Jews and Judaism have, for much of Christian theological speculation, functioned as the quintessential Other, the catalyst whereby Christianity has both defined itself and articulated its doctrines. Christian supersessionism was and still is predicated on the notion that Judaism was a dead religion defined by legalism as opposed to the spirit and has no relevance after the advent of Jesus, whose message included the best and most universal aspects of ancient Israel's prophetic tradition. It is perhaps no wonder, then, that Judaism has occupied an ambiguous position within the academic study of religion, a discipline that some contend further reifies Christian categories and makes them the standard by which all other religions (not just Judaism) are judged and found wanting (e.g., Dubuisson 2003, 105). Whereas these other religious traditions (e.g., Buddhism, Taoism, Confucianism, Hinduism) are safely removed from the so-called "Western" traditions, Judaism (much like Islam, but for different reasons) has always occupied a problematic position from the perspective of Christianity. Indeed for much of the nineteenth century and the majority of the first half of the twentieth century, Judaism was only taught, even at so-called "secular" institutions, insofar as it provided the backdrop to Jesus and the early Christian movement. This must certainly be taken into consideration against charges that Jewish studies is somehow "too ethnic" or "too apologetic." In many ways, given its tenuous history examined in the previous two chapters, this should not strike us as all that surprising as Jewish scholars aided by the munificence of Jewish communities have had to fight for the inclusion of Jewish topics at universities. The task ahead for the discipline, as I have mentioned several times in this study, is to move beyond such apologetics and special pleading.

Indicative of the supersessionist argument, Frank Ellinwood, professor of comparative religions at the University of the City of New York (soon to be renamed New York University) and a Presbyterian minister wrote in his *Oriental Religions and Christianity* (1892): "And I am cheered with a belief that, in proportion to the intelligent discrimination which shall be exercised in judging of the non-Christian religions, and the skill which shall be shown in presenting the immensely superior truths of the Christian faith, will the success of the great work of Missions be increased" (Ellinwood 1892, 2). Here Ellinwood makes clear that his aim of comparison is anything but neutral, but predicated on (Protestant) Christian supremacy. His comments also reveal to just what uses the so-called "objective" comparative study of religion could be and were put. Indeed, this has always been a problem for the academic study of Judaism in departments of religious studies. The latter's assumptions and presuppositions are inherently predisposed against certain forms of religion and religious practices (Orsi 2005, 2–12). Comments such as Ellinwood's are certainly not unique to this time period. In fact, as argued in chapter 2, it is such comments—and the hermeneutic that informs them—that were largely responsible for keeping the academic study of Jewish topics out of German universities before the early twentieth century.

Such comments, moreover, have played a huge role in the various ways that Judaism has been situated both within and without the academy, and both within and without Jewish studies.

In the rest of this chapter, I wish to examine some of the key figures responsible for trying to integrate the academic study of Judaism and religion in the twentieth century—their assumptions, tensions, and fractures. For the sake of convenience, I focus solely on the American context because it is here, more than anywhere, that Jewish studies has largely been conceived in tandem with the academic study of religion. In so doing, the present chapter continues the discussion and analysis of the previous chapter, moving from the general to the more specific.

As we should come to expect, these case studies by no means provide a uniform narrative. This is fitting given the many different methodological approaches and even personal backgrounds of the individuals under consideration. Indeed, this lack of uniformity further attests to one of the central arguments of this study; namely, that there is no simple way to classify Jewish studies in the North American academy. Whereas some want to write it off as too apologetical, as a special interest discipline, or as an ethnic enclave, the fact is that while it can function—and, indeed, has functioned—as all of these, none of these exhausts the possible configuration of what Jewish studies either has been or can be. As the individuals examined in these case studies clearly display, each one provides a different narrative of what Judaism is based on the particular circumstances of their own personal and intellectual backgrounds. Some of these scholars, as we shall see, are ethnically Jewish (e.g., Morris Jastrow, Jacob Neusner, J. Z. Smith), whereas others are non-Jews (e.g., George Foot Moore, Erwin Goodenough). This religio-ethnic difference, however, does *not* lead into tidy bifurcations, as we might be accustomed to believe, wherein the latter tend to be more critical than the former. On the contrary, ethnic background played little role in determining how each one of these individuals either conceived of or taxonomized Judaism. The thread that unites them is that all work on premodern forms of Judaism, choosing to focus their attention on either biblical or postbiblical (i.e., rabbinic) forms. Indeed, this focus on the late antique or medieval period—and I think it safe to generalize, especially given the analysis in chapter 2—is a common feature of the academic study of Judaism until fairly recently.[9] Moreover, it also reinforces the biases introduced by Wissenschaft des Judentums, examined in chapter 2.

Example 1: Morris Jastrow Jr. (1861–1921)

Morris Jastrow Jr. was one of the earliest individuals in the United States who was interested in the secular and nondenominational study of religion. His interest in Jewish data, however, was more complicated. He only tended to make reference to the latter when it suited him, primarily because his theory of religion was interested in "primitive" religious forms from the ancient Near East, a milieu from which the religion of ancient Israel, for various ideological reasons, had largely been excluded. So, despite the fact that Jastrow was a strong advocate for the historical and nondenominational study of religion within the secular university, he was often unwilling to apply such methods to Judaism, his own religion. This, for lack of a better term, "double standard" is not uncommon in the study of religion,[10] wherein that which one holds dear for personal or religious reasons can be neatly removed or excepted from critical analysis.

Morris Jastrow Jr. was the son of the famed rabbi and Talmudic scholar, Marcus Jastrow, who was the author of an important lexicon of rabbinic literature. The young Morris was educated at the University of Pennsylvania, before traveling to Europe to complete his studies. He studied at numerous universities there, working with some of the most important figures in the German historical and Orientalist traditions. In Breslau, for example, he studied at the revolutionary rabbinical seminary founded by Zacharias Frankel, wherein both Heinrich Graetz and David Rosin taught;[11] at Leipzig, he worked with Franz and Frederick (father and son) Delitzsch, the latter being an Assyriolygist and the former a Hebraist;[12] at Straßburg, he studied with the famed Arabist and Quranic scholar Theordor Nöldeke; and at Paris he studied with, among others, the Orientalist Ernest Renan (Clay and Montgomery 1921, x). He received his PhD in 1884 from the University of Leipzig for a dissertation entitled "Abu Zakarijja Jahja b. Dawud Hajjug und Seine Zwei Grammatischen Schriften über die Verben mit Schwachen Buchstaben und die Verben mit Doppelbuchstaben" (1885), which examined a series of unpublished grammatical works by the Judeo-Arabic grammarian Judah ben David al-Hayyuj (ca. 945–ca. 1000). Jastrow would go on to become a prolific scholar, president of the American Oriental Society (AOS) from 1914 through 1915, and president of the Society of Biblical Literature (SBL) in 1916.

In Europe, Jastrow seems to have been heavily influenced by the Religionsgeschichte Schule, which became popular in Germany in the late nineteenth-century (Simon 1975, 135). Religionsgeschichte, among other things, emphasized the relationship between religious texts and cultural contexts and included the application of historical-critical method to texts that had previously been regarded as sacred or eternal. It was a revolutionary approach that changed the way that many looked at the biblical text, both the Old and New Testaments, but certainly one that was not without its fair share of controversy. In Europe, as David Myers argues, the repercussions of these debates over how to read biblical texts "properly"—that is, historically or religiously—created a virtual *Kulturkampf* (Myers 2003, 30–34).

Upon his return to America, Jastrow was instrumental in founding the Committee of American Lectures on the History of Religions (ALHR), and he remained its secretary until his death. He also became the general editor of the *Series of Handbooks on the History of Religions*, wherein his *Religion of Babylon and Assyria* appeared as the second volume (Barton 1921, 327–28). Under his general editorship, such pioneering classics as Edward Washburn Hopkins, *Religions of India* (1896), and Crawford Howell Toy, *Introduction to the History of Religions* (1913), appeared.

Within this context, it is certainly worth noting the significant change between Marcus the father and Morris the son. Whereas the father was European born and educated—recalling that it would have been impossible for him to have an academic career, even had he wanted to—he engaged privately in academic interests, publishing his magnum opus, *A Dictionary of the Targumim, the Talmud Babli and Yerushalmi, and the Midrashic Literature* (2005 [1903]), a work that to this day remains an important resource. Morris, the son, however, seems to have consciously opted out of a rabbinic career in favor of a scholarly one. Despite this, university authorities, colleagues, and community members frequently viewed Jastrow and those like him as rabbis rather than scholars because their primary object of study was the ancient Near East (which included ancient Israel).

In 1902, Jastrow published a generalist work, *The Study of Religion*, which appeared in a new series entitled *The Contemporary Science Series*, edited by Havelock Ellis, the English psychologist and student of human sexuality. Jastrow dedicated this volume to one of his mentors, the famed historian of religions Cornelius Tiele (1830–1902), who had been instrumental in arguing for the inclusion of Religionsgeschichte in Dutch universities, something that had recently passed through an act of the Dutch Parliament.[13] In the preface to the work, Jastrow makes his own position on the matter clear:

> I take my stand therefore as an advocate of the historical method in the study of religion as the condition *sine qua*

non for any results of enduring character, no matter what
the particular aspect of religion it be that engages our attention. Whatever the defects of the exposition may be, it will,
I trust, at least justify the correctness of the general position
here taken. It is my earnest hope also, in some measure to
contribute through this book to the more general interest
in the historical study of religions. (Jastrow 1902, ix)

Jastrow here articulates a problem that resides at the heart of the academic study of religion in general and that of Judaism in particular:
despite religion's appeals to the life of the spirit and its inherently
personal dimension, Jastrow contends that its academic study must
be nonpartisan. The academic study of religion, in other words, is
neither about catechesis nor proselytization, but about historical and
philological study. Yet, in imagining Judaism as but one among many
other religions as opposed to the chosen or elect, Jastrow—caught in
the trap like many discussed in the previous chapter—would inevitably have run up against the censure of many of his coreligionists,
undoubtedly including his own father. Whether for this or other reasons, Jastrow primarily refrained from studying Jewish data. If Jews
and Judaism are historicized, they become one more people among
other peoples and one more religion among other religions. According to Jastrow,

It is but a proper concession due to the direct interest that
Christians of all denominations, and Jews, whether orthodox
or advanced, have in the presentation of their religious history that the greatest possible care be exercised to secure for
the subject an impartial, strictly historical, and at the same
time sympathetic treatment. In setting forth the doctrines
and rites of Judaism and Christianity, there is no need of
any discussion of their value, but merely of their historical
aspects. Indeed such discussion should be rigidly excluded,
and similarly, in unfolding the development of the religion
of the ancient Hebrews, all doctrinal questions should be
left to one side. (358)

Jastrow's call here is both an early and an important one for objectivity in the academic study of religion—despite that fact that he never
quite articulates what he means by a "sympathetic" treatment and
how this can square with a disinterested historical one. This type of
historical study, which he argues must include the study of Jewish

and Christian forms, must be introduced as the nontheological academic study of religion within colleges and universities throughout
the United States. The goal of such an introduction, according to him,
will be an understanding that "the historical study of religions [ought
to become] a subject admissible as a major or minor" (375). Although I
do think flagging in this context that what Jastrow proposes—the historical *and* sympathetic study of religion—may well be an oxymoron.
A sympathetic treatment will, after all, tend to diminish or marginalize those historical aspects that make us potentially uncomfortable or
threaten the sympathetic taxonomies that we have created.

In his *Aspects of Religious Belief and Practice in Babylonia and Assyria* (1911)—the eighth volume of American Lectures on the History
of Religions—Jastrow examines, as the title indicates, the religious
beliefs and practices of the ancient Babylonians and Assyrians. His
reason for doing so, as he makes clear in his preface to the work is
as follows: "I have, therefore, availed myself of this opportunity to
present in outline a picture of the chief deities in the systematized
pantheon, with due regard to the manner in which the original traits
of these deities were overlaid with the attributes accorded to them
because of the political position assumed by the centers in which they
were worshipped" (1911, vi). Jastrow's major concern in this book is
not the religious forms of ancient Israel, but those found among its
neighbors. This is interesting for several reasons. It shows that Jastrow
did not simply gravitate to "Jewish topics" of the ancient Near East
because he himself happened to be Jewish. Although we might well
wish he had given the general supersessionist hermeneutic supplied
by the likes of Frank Ellinwood, mentioned above, or some of those
individuals that I shall discuss presently. Indeed Jastrow seems to
have been decidedly uninterested in what we might label Jewish data,
preferring instead to focus his attentions and energy on other religions
and cultures of the region. His reason for this, as he makes clear in
an essay from 1899, that is, well before he published his works on
the religious forms of Babylonia and Assyria, was that such religions
better permit us to understand how religion works:

> Advanced religions like Christianity, Judaism, Islam, and
> Buddhism offer comparatively little opportunity for inves-
> tigating the fundamental problems in religions viewed as
> a part of man's life. For understanding such problems we
> must turn to religions that are more naïve, which are less
> the result of conscious effort, in which speculation plays
> a minor part, which, in a word are *direct* manifestations

of man's emotional and religious nature. The religion of
savages and of people living in a primitive condition of
culture are the more special concern of the student of
religion. (1899, 318)

Here Jastrow—following the likes of Tylor, Frazier, Durkheim, and
many other contemporaneous theorists of religion—contends that to
understand the religious imagination, including its origins and evolution, one must study the religious expressions of either ancient religions or modern "savages" and "primitives" (Eilberg-Schwartz 1990,
1–28). These types of religions, as Jastrow makes clear in the above
passage, presumably permit a more direct access into the religious
imagination because they represent purer or more pristine expressions,
thereby allowing the interpreter to encounter what more "advanced"
religions cover up with, for example, ritualization or theological jus-
tification. Despite its antiquity, however, ancient Judaism is usually
exempted from such an analysis because, for Christian scholars, it
necessarily formed the general milieu out of which the "ultimate" religious form, that is, Christianity, emerged. And, for many Jewish scholars, ancient Judaism represented the core of their own religion, and
because of this, there was a tendency not to draw parallels between
Judaism and the religions of the so-called "savages" (Eilberg-Schwartz
1990, 3). There is an impulse among both Jewish and Christian writ-
ers in the late nineteenth and early twentieth centuries, in the words
of Howard Eilberg-Schwartz, to "radically differentiate Judaism and
savage religions [that] was part of an ongoing attempt to protect the
privileged status of Judaism, and by extension, Christianity" (1990, 3).

Jastrow, then, primarily studied Assyrian and Babylonian religions, claiming that when it comes "to the religions of the past, no
conflict with current religious sentiments is conceivable" (1912, 355).
Occasionally Jastrow will use these primitive religious forms as a way
of making comparisons with that of the ancient Israelites as found
in the Hebrew Bible. However, this occurs only rarely, and he seems
to be quite content to study the former religions on their own terms.

For Jastrow, as we have seen, any questions of doctrine or truth
had no place in the classroom. The study of religion was, for him,
little different than the study of history, economics, or philosophy.
Even though he wrote and published his doctoral dissertation on
the medieval grammar of al-Hayyuj, his later career saw him largely
avoid aspects of Judaism. Despite Jastrow's presence at the University
of Pennsylvania, the academic study of Judaism was largely nonex-
istent at this institution (Ritterband and Wechsler 1994, 191). Indeed,

as one of Jastrow's colleagues remarked following his death, "We have touched upon many religions [in the Committee on the History of Religions]; I could never get Jastrow to take up Judaism" (qtd. in Ritterband and Wechsler 1994, 191).

Among the other early presenters in the American Lectures on the History of Religions, two are also worth singling out. In marked contrast to Jastrow, these individuals were particularly interested in the religion of ancient Israel; however neither was interested in it *after* the time of Jesus. The two individuals in question and their published lectures were Thomas Kelly Cheyne, *Jewish Religious Life after the Exile* (1898), and Karl Budde, *Religion of Israel to the Exile* (1899). Both Cheyne and Budde were Christian theologians, although the former was certainly more controversial than the latter. T. K. Cheyne (1841–1915) was born in London, trained in biblical criticism in Germany (Göttingen), became an Anglican priest, and was installed as the Oriel Professor of the Interpretation of Holy Scripture in 1885, a position that carried with it the canonry of Rochester. Interestingly in 1912, near the end of his life, he switched religious allegiances and became a member of the Baha'i faith, something that his official obituary in the *New York Times* fails to mention.[14] Indeed, Cheyne became the most eminent Western academic to convert to Baha'i in the early twentieth century (Lambden n.d.). Karl Ferdinand Reinhardt Budde (1850–1935) was born in the North Westphalia Region of Germany, and, whereas Cheyne went form Britain to Germany to receive his academic training, Budde went from Germany to Britain, where he completed his Doctor of Divinity at the University of St. Andrews in Scotland. He was appointed professor of Old Testament exegesis and biblical Hebrew at the University of Marburg in 1900, which would have made him an older colleague of Rudolf Otto.

Cheyne, writing before his conversion to the Baha'i religion, sets for himself two goals in his lectures. The primary one, as he himself makes clear, is to try to provide his general audience with an understanding of "the history of our mother-religion" (1898, xix) and "to stimulate a more general appreciation of Jewish piety" (1898, xx). And although Cheyne's work provides its audience with a great deal of historical data, his conclusion to the work makes clear both his own orientation and the personal or theological reasons behind his academic interest in the data supplied by the postexilic period:

> But before I conclude, let me urge upon you not to let these historical inquiries languish. If there are other voices which sound more enticing to the men and women of this

generation, it does not follow that they are really more important than the call to search the Scriptures. Religious reform is a necessary condition of social progress and with a view to this the origin and nature of essential Christianity, and—shall I add??—of essential Judaism, has to be investigated afresh. Deeply as it stirs our feelings, none of us should refuse to take part in the grave debate. I do not undervalue the study of the early Israelitish religion; indeed, I could wish to have included its records within my survey. *But it is the study of the religious formation which developed out of this which has the most claim on our attention, because of its close relation to the historical problem of early Christianity.* (1898, 261; my italics)

Here Cheyne argues that his investigation into the historical materials of the postexilic period (from the time of the building of the second temple in ca. 530 BCE to 70 CE) is necessary because it helps to illumine the spiritual and religious teachings of Jesus and what will be the eventual emergence of the early Christian Church. The postexilic period, in other words, is significant insofar as it provides insight into the historical *and theological* problems associated with the rise of early Christianity (see Smith 1990). Once again, we see here the conflation of history and theology, despite the call of those like Jastrow to keep them apart from one another. The historical study of ancient Israel provides the vehicle by which to understand the meaning of what Cheyne calls "essential Judaism"—that is, the inner heart or core of Judaism that proves "essential" for the emergence of Christianity. This heart presumably departs from Judaism after the advent of Jesus, leaving a hollow shell of a religion. There is no desire to trace this "essential" nature in any Jewish forms after the destruction of the temple in 70 CE because the "real" Israel, that is, its true essence, has been channeled into Christianity. It is the latter that Cheyne calls "the efflorescence of the religious spirit of Judaism" (1898, 261). Although Cheyne may differ from Jastrow in both his religious obligation and his intellectual hermeneutic, they both share the opinion—albeit for radically different reasons—that Judaism after the destruction of the second temple period is largely uninteresting.

In Karl Budde's lectures, published in the year after those of Cheyne, the interest switches to the preexilic history (from roughly the origins to the destruction of the first temple in 587 BCE) of ancient Israel. According to Budde, as he sets it up in his preface, the goal of the biblical critic of the Old Testament is to show the progression from the Old to the New: "If the shortest possible line was to be drawn between the starting-point and the goal, it must be all the clearer that this line is a straight one, that the way by which the unique development of the religion of Israel progressed, notwithstanding all apparent deflection and zig-zags, really led consistently, necessarily, wisely, and triumphantly upward, and at that point where these lectures stop already opens a vista of the consummation in the Gospel of Jesus Christ" (1899, xvi). Framed more explicitly than in Cheyne's lectures, Budde here makes clear that the consummate religious expression of the material that he presents will only occur centuries later. Writing as a Christian theologian, he subsequently clarifies his aim is not to present his audience with criticism of the Old Testament that is written "from the negative side" (1899, xvi). On the contrary it is to show how this religious document articulates itself "in a truly living organism" (1899, xvi). The flipside of the "living" religion is that the other religion that claims the Old Testament as its own is somehow "dead." What follows is a set of six lectures devoted to the manifold religious forms associated with ancient Israel, with an eye on how they find ultimate fulfillment in the figure of Jesus Christ.

Budde is quick to find in the material produced by the ancient Israelites a universalist message, what he occasionally refers to as "the religion of Yahweh," that is "destined to become the religion of all mankind" (1899, 216). This "religion of Yahweh," as he informs us in a note on the first page of the first lecture, was "at first crude, [but] grew constantly in purity and elevation till at last, in the progress of revelation, [it] reached the lofty spirituality of the New Testament" (1899, 1). However, there are, according to him, kernels of this lofty, universal aspect found in prophetic books such as Deutero-Isaiah and Micah. Despite the existence of this universalism in such books, he subsequently argues, this religion "was not at that time fulfilled, and [their] extravagant promises retired into the background for a long time under the pressure of the post-exilic conditions of Jewish life" (1899, 216). Such a message, not surprising given his own religious and professional proclivities, would—indeed could—only find its fulfillment in the coming of Jesus Christ and his messianic prophecy that would build naturally upon the universalism of Isaiah, particularly Deutero-Isaiah. This universalism, in Budde's eyes, was able to transcend naturally the particularism found in more "ritualistic" or "legal" books (presumably those like Leviticus and Deuteronomy). He writes in the grand conclusion to his lecture series,

> Can we conceive of any sharper contrasts than we find
> between the world-wide, glowing universalism of Deutero-
> Isaiah and the narrow, icy particularism of Ezekiel—between
> the ritualism of Ezekiel and the complete superiority of
> Jeremiah and Deutero-Isaiah to all external cult—between
> the resignation of Jeremiah and the enthusiastic expectations
> of the other two—between the inner life of God in Jeremiah
> and the world-wide sublimity of the God of Ezekiel? . . . It
> has pleased God to His human children the noblest and
> most beautiful flower of His revelation, the Gospel of His
> Son Jesus Christ. (1899, 218)

For Budde, as the passage clearly demonstrates, studying the religion
of ancient Israel is not an end in and of itself. The religion of the
ancient Israelites is sketched (1) to provide the ancient roots of Jesus'
message and, in the process, (2) to show the ultimate uniqueness of
that message. Judaism was of interest to Budde and many scholars
like him, as the foil of Christianity. This must always be kept in mind
when Judaism has been situated intellectually within the academy.
This genealogy also illumines why the academic study of Judaism,
for better or worse, largely remains in the hands of Jewish scholars
to this day and why it possesses a tendency toward apologetics. For
Budde, reflecting the opinion of many scholars and theologians of
his day, the particularist message of Judaism ceases to be a religion
in the aftermath of the destruction of the second temple in 70 CE.
For those like Budde, this was largely because it failed to recognize
its own inclusive message (something that Christianity was successfully able to do) and instead followed the ritualistic and exclusive
one. Judaism is only of interest as the backdrop, context, and milieu
of Jesus' messianic fulfillment. Again, it is worth pointing out that
Budde's highly apologetic account occurs under the auspices of a
series devoted to American Lectures on the *History of Religions* (my
italics). Despite claims to objectivity in both the title of the series in
which Budde's monograph appears and the general claims to disinterest in the discipline of the history of religions or religious studies (or
whatever else we want to call it), what we witness are supersessionist
apologetics in the guise of academic objectivity,

The juxtaposition of Jastrow with Cheyne and Budde is striking.
Whereas the latter two are completely uninterested in postbiblical
Judaism and only interested in the biblical period insofar as it illu-
mines another religion, the former is interested in how the religions of
Babylonia and Assyria occasionally illumine biblical forms. All three

situate Judaism against the backdrop of competing agendas—whether to imply the uniqueness of Judaism (Jastrow) or its transcendence by Christianity (Cheyne and Budde). We have seen both of these agendas time and again in this study. They are, moreover, agendas that we continue to see, albeit now in slightly different guises.

Example 2: George Foot Moore (1851–1931)

There is a danger, one perhaps reinforced by the previous section, in assuming that every Jewish scholar of the ancient Near East will necessarily be an apologist for Judaism and that, concomitantly, every Christian scholar must, by definition, be a supersessionist or, at the very least, a Christian apologist. George Foot Moore provides an excellent case study that shatters such unwarranted assumptions. As both a Presbyterian minister and professor of Hebrew and the history of religions at Harvard, George Foot Moore perhaps did more than anyone in these early years, *including Morris Jastrow*, to show that Judaism possessed a dynamic history beyond the destruction of the second temple in 70 CE. Moore seems to have been, for example, the first person at a secular institution in the United States to have both developed and taught a course devoted to Judaism as a living tradition and not simply as a backdrop to the emergence of Christianity (Ritterband and Wechsler 1994, 191).

Like Jastrow, Moore was heavily influenced by the textual and contextual approach afforded by the German school of Religions-geschichte and sought to apply its methods in his own research. However, whereas Jastrow was almost completely uninterested in postbiblical Judaism, preferring instead to study the religious forms of cognate cultures, Moore's primary area of interest was in the period immediately after the codification of the Bible. In particular, he spent a great deal of intellectual effort elucidating what he considered to be the dynamic and rich thought produced by the rabbis between the third and fifth centuries CE.

Among his many monographs devoted to the academic study of religion, Moore published a two-volume work devoted to providing a historical study of the world's religions entitled *The History of Religions*. In the second volume, subtitled *Judaism, Christianity, Mohammedanism*, he strikes a somewhat different tone than witnessed in the superses-sionist hermeneutics of those such as Cheyne or Budde. In his preface to the second volume, for example, Moore attempts to show the inter-connections among the three religions, writing that they

> are so intimately related to one another that in a morphologi-
> cal classification they might be regarded as three branches
> of monotheistic religion in Western Asia and Europe.
> Christianity originated in a religious movement in Judaism,
> and a Jewish Messianic sect, and though it soon separated
> from the parent stock, and in the gentile world became
> a universal redemptive religion, it was to its inheritance
> from Judaism, that it chiefly owed its religious and moral
> superiority. Mohammedanism owes its existence to the
> impression Jewish and, in smaller degree, Christian ideas
> made upon the mind of the Arabian prophet. (1919, vii)

Here we see little of the supersessionism that appeared in the lectures
of Cheyne and Budde. Instead, Moore seeks to contextualize each religion in its historical setting without seeking to demonstrate, as was so
customary at the time, how the universal trends of ancient Judaism
naturally lead into the Jesus event that is paradoxically characterized as
"unique" from its immediate surroundings (see Hughes 2013). Indeed,
in Moore's volume—which is divided chronologically into three parts,
each of which is devoted to one of the particular monotheisms—we
witness a good one-half of his description of Judaism devoted to postbiblical Judaism and its many sources. Whereas chapters 1 and 2 are
devoted to ancient Judaism, chapter 3 is entitled "School and Synagogue," which examines post-biblical and rabbinic developments, and
chapter 4 is entitled "Judaism: Medieval and Modern."

In the third chapter, devoted to the collection and redaction of
rabbinic materials, Moore's hermeneutic is clearly on display. Whereas
the great majority of Christian interpreters—from the late antique period to the present—had either largely denied a post-Temple existence
to Judaism or had reduced it to uninteresting legalism, Moore explores
rabbinic Judaism in considerable detail. Despite the years of persecu-
tion under both the Persian and Byzantine Empires, Moore argues that
rabbinic commentary and texts provide "evidence that the moral and
religious teaching of earlier times was kept alive" (1919, 80).

Moore would devote much of his subsequent work to this period of Jewish cultural and intellectual florescence in the late antique
period. In 1927, Moore published his three-volume *Judaism in the First
Centuries of the Christian Era: The Age of the Tannaim*. In this work,
he seeks to "represent Judaism in the centuries in which it assumed
its definitive form as it presents itself in the tradition which it has
always regarded as authentic" (1955 [1927], vii). Again, this is a far

cry from the more traditional one that regards Judaism as essentially ending with the destruction of the Temple in 70 CE. Instead, Moore can write that it was in these early centuries of the Common Era that

> Judaism brought to complete development its characteristic institutions, the school and the synagogue, in which it possessed not only a unique instrument for the education and edification of all classes of the people in religion and morality, but the center of its religious life, and to no small extent also of its intellectual and social life. Through the study of the Scriptures and the discussions of generations of scholars it defined its religious conceptions, its moral principles, its forms of worship, and its distinctive type of piety, as well as the rules of law and observance which became authoritative for all succeeding time. (1955 [1927], 1)

For Moore, Judaism in the postbiblical period possessed its own unique structure that was not necessarily apparent in the biblical materials. In addition to writing about these postbiblical trends in Judaism, Moore also introduced the study of Judaism into the Harvard curriculum, teaching—as we have seen—what was probably the first class on Judaism as a living tradition within the auspices of the History of Religions Program. However, as Ritterband and Wechsler point out, while Harvard was committed to George Foot Moore, it was not necessarily committed to the academic study of Judaism (1994, 193). Once Moore retired from the faculty, for example, his successor, Arthur Darby Nock, was a scholar of Christianity not Judaism, and the latter ceased to be taught in the way that Moore had conceived of it.

Example 3: Erwin Ramsdell Goodenough (1893–1965)

Erwin Goodenough was, like Moore, a non-Jew. He was a New Testament scholar by training and, in particular, a scholar of Philo and Hellenistic Judaism, at Yale University where he taught from 1923 through 1962. Goodenough is primarily known for his massive thirteen-volume *Jewish Symbols in the Greco-Roman Period* (1953–1968). In this work, Goodenough collected all of what he considered to be the iconographic remains from the ancient and early late antique world (the so-called Greco-Roman period), with the aim of showing that, contrary to contemporaneous rabbinic accounts, popular Judaism was most interested in mysticism and salvation, two themes that were very common in the various mystery cults and religions of the period, including, of course, Christianity (Levine 1998, 8).

For Goodenough, the religious forms produced by Jews in the late antique period can only be understood within the context of the larger cultures in which Jews happened to find themselves. One of his major theses was that popular Judaism in these early centuries largely rejected the authority of the "official" Judaism produced by the rabbis (see Schwartz 2002, 98–99). Goodenough was roundly attacked by other scholars for his reliance on Jungian interpretation of the artistic symbols in question and his desire to remove the rabbis from "Greco-Roman" influence. Nevertheless, his argument that scholars of the period need to take into consideration both text and context, in addition to the methodological problems of reconstructing these early periods, would prove both important and influential; in this regard his two major intellectual disciples would be Morton Smith and Jacob Neusner (Schwartz 2002).

For all its theoretical and hermeneutical shortcomings, it seems that Goodenough's approach—his ability to speak to other religionists working with other data sets from cognate religious traditions—was instrumental in subsequent efforts to get the study of Judaism taught in departments of religious studies in the 1960s and 1970s. A large part of Goodenough's success was the result of his work being pub-lished by the Bollingen foundation, funded by Paul Mellon—one of the great art collectors of the twentieth century—and named after the village in Switzerland where Carl Gustav Jung had a rural retreat. The initial goal of the foundation was to ensure as wide an audience as possible for Jung's works. In the words of Paul Mellon, "The idea of the Collected Works of Jung might be considered the central core, the binding factor, not only of the Foundation's general direction but also of the ultimate intellectual temper of the Bollingen Series as a whole."[15] The result was the publication of books, many of which were somehow related to Jung's vision of the unconscious, by scholars associated with his Eranos Conference in Ascona, Switzerland (see Wasserstrom 1999, 24–25) and published in distinguished series at Princeton University Press.

Perhaps it was no coincidence that as Goodenough's vision of Jewish symbols, tied as they were to the then in-vogue Jungian arche-types, reached a large audience, Jewish studies began to draw new life in religious studies departments. It was during these years, write Ritterband and Wechsler, that "the study of Judaism within religion departments had found its niche, adopted the rhetoric and methodologies of secular critics, differentiated its domain from that of theology, claimed to illumine general religious phenomena, and reserved for itself an internal integrity" (1994, 198). This movement from Semitics to religious studies in the 1960s and 1970s was significant for two reasons: first, as we saw in the previous chapter, it became intertwined with identity politics and the discourses of inclusion. Second, and equally important, it created a switch in constituencies. Whereas Semitics consisted of, for the most part, graduate programs (often associated with Seminary training) at private institutions, religious studies was soon to become a staple of the American undergraduate curriculum.

Example 4: Jacob Neusner (1932–)

Jacob Neusner has perhaps done more than anyone to integrate the academic study of Judaism within the larger disciplinary canopy of religious studies. He received (Conservative) rabbinic ordination at the Jewish Theological Seminary (JTS) in 1960, and then his PhD from Columbia University in 1961 under the guidance of Salo Wittmayer Baron and Morton Smith. Despite his massive number of publications (as many as eight hundred books),[16] many of which are both repetitive and vituperative (see, e.g., Neusner 1995),[17] his work—especially his early work—was responsible for redefining the academic study of Judaism.

In his early writings, Neusner's goal was to show simultaneously both the complexity and the basic structure of rabbinic Judaism. Rather than regard all of rabbinic Judaism as a monolithic religious movement, however, Neusner prefers to envisage the various texts produced as individual pieces of data that illumine local Judaisms at particular times and places. For Neusner, then, these texts represented but one aspect of manifold religious traditions that often were in competition with one another. This movement from rabbinic Judaism to Neusner's conception of rabbinic Judaisms would switch focus from normativity to complexity.

In a revised version of his dissertation, *A Life of Yohanan ben Zakkai*, Neusner informs us that, unlike his predecessors, he seeks to reevaluate our understanding of what rabbinic texts can and cannot tell us:

Here my task is critically to study and analyse these sources
[on Yohanan ben Zakkai], to try and locate the origins of
different parts of them, to see how the whole structure grew.
My purpose in this is not to produce a connected history of
the man and his time, but to offer systematic observations
on the tradition about him and through it, on the development of a sample body of Talmudic literature. . . . I do not
suppose we can come to a final and positive assessment
of the historicity of various stories and sayings. We surely
cannot declare a narrative to be historically reliable simply
because it contains no improbabilities . . . We must not
confuse verisimilitudes with authenticity. (1970, xi)

Earlier generations of scholars, especially those in Israel, had largely
accepted rabbinic documents at face value when it came to their historicity. This led them to believe that, historiographically, they could
reconstruct earlier periods with accuracy. Neusner's hermeneutic here
undermines this project. For him, the self-conscious scholar of rabbinic materials has to be cautious of whether or not he could ever
uncover historical information from the religious laws and anecdotes
told by earlier generations, especially those in the late antique period.
Neusner's skepticism undercut the traditional scholarly genre of biographical composition of these rabbis and instead shifted "from the
content of the traditions to the historical factors affecting their trans-
missions" (Schwartz 2004, 104).

Although Neusner's insights are in danger of being eclipsed by
the sheer volume and repetition in his later works, his basic notion
that we cannot take rabbinic accounts at face value and his insistence
that rabbinic Judaism represented only one variety of manifold Judaisms are very important (and here we see his indebtedness to Goodenough). It might be worth quoting from one of his most important
works, *Judaism: The Evidence of the Mishnah* (1988). Reacting against
George Foot Moore's *Judaism in the First Centuries of the Common Era*,
Neusner articulates his own hermeneutic and his own account in light
of criticizing his predecessor:

[Moore's work] is . . . not really a work in the history
of religions at all, in this instance, the socially grounded,
developmental, and formative history of a particular brand
of Judaism. His research is into theology. It is organized
in theological categories, not differentiated by historical
periods at all . . . Moore makes no pretense of account-

ing systematically for development and change. What is constructed is a static exercise in dogmatic theology, not an account of the history of religious ideas or—still more urgent—the society of a people who held these ideas. . . . He does not explore the interplay between that worldview and the historical and political context of the community that held it. In so far as history attends to the material context of ideas and the social perspectives expressed by ideas and institutions alike, in so far as ideas are deemed part of a larger social system, and systems held to be pertinent to the given political and economic framework which contains them, Moore's account of dogmatic theology has nothing to do with religious history—the history of Judaism or of one kind of Judaism in the first two centuries of the Common Era. (1988, 8)

As this passage makes clear, Neusner's novelty is that he refuses simply to describe the contents of rabbinic texts, preferring instead to analyze and taxonomize them. In so doing, he argues that we ought to inquire into the social, material, economic, and historical conditions that made such texts possible in the first place. This movement from description to analysis, from contents to structure, signals an important marker in the developing relationship between the academic study of religion and Jewish data (see, e.g., Neusner 1979). These rabbinic texts are now to be approached using a set of issues (e.g., the social construction to reality) that those working with other datasets in other religious traditions should be able to understand.

Example 5: Jonathan Z. Smith (1938–)

Jonathan Z. Smith, a historian of religions at the University of Chicago, is perhaps one of the best-known and most influential figures currently working on issues of theory and method within the academic study of religion. Despite his theoretical erudition and his manifold interest in various cultures, his primary dataset is early Judaism and its fluid relationship both to early Christianity and other religious forms of the late antique period. Not unlike Neusner, Smith calls for an extreme level of self-consciousness and self-reflexivity in the scholar of religion (e.g., 1974, 1–5).

Smith is most preoccupied with the fluid borders between early Judaisms and early Christianities; the criteria we use to differentiate them from one another; and the extrascholarly desiderata that lead us to the comparative enterprise that examines Judaism and Christianity in the first place. Defining anything, let alone something as gargantuan and complex as a "religion," Smith argues, is neither an easy nor a straightforward matter. Using early Judaism as his *exemplum*, Smith claims that even the act of simply or categorically defining something such as ancient Judaism demands a complex or polythetic system of classification. Given the available historical evidence of something we now call "ancient Judaism" in addition to the methodological problems inherent to definition and classification, Smith argues that there can exist no one "differential quality" that marks Jews from non-Jews. However, the persistence remains to define ancient Judaism and to make it distinct from other religions of late antiquity using monothetic terms. These efforts, writes Smith, "have not been convincing; they have failed to achieve a consensus. They have been poorly formulated and violate the ordinary canons of definition. But this is less disturbing than the fact that the presuppositions of the monothetic enterprise have been deliberately tampered with for apologetic reasons" (1974, 5). This deliberate tampering emerges from the desire, both scholarly and nonscholarly, to construct our data as somehow unique.

As a result, the pursuit for a "normative Judaism" (or a "normative" anything) tends to ignore all those data-sets (historical evidence, material remains, and so one) that fly in the face of such a constructed normativity. This is not just about diversity within religious traditions; it gets to the very heart of the conceptual difficulties inherent to the act of defining. Employing a polythetic mode of taxonomy to define an ancient Jew, for example, need not be dependent upon any single marker of belief or practice (e.g., circumcision or synagogue attendance). On the contrary, all an ancient Jew need do is adhere to some, more than a non-Jew, of the defining features of so-called "Jewish identity." An ancient Jew, then, might speak Greek, be uncircumcised, and be uninterested in attending a synagogue, yet still identify as a Jew. Defining this ancient Jew (or anyone else) tells us very little, at least a priori, about which taxonomic indices define such an individual.

Smith's work—its attention to overlapping taxa, the shared or blurred boundaries, and showing the ideology of interpretations when it comes to later understandings by Christian apologists—has proved highly influential. Let me briefly mention within this context the work of Daniel Boyarin. Boyarin is not a student of Smith; however, like the latter, he is a highly self-conscious student of the religious forms of the late antique period. Boyarin's work, which I shall discuss in greater detail in chapter 6, is interested in the shared border separating Judaism and Christianity in the early centuries CE. Borderlines, he reminds us, are there for a reason: to keep apart those groups that bear the most family resemblances to one another. In so doing he writes,

> Groups that are differentiated in various ways by class, ethnicity, and other forms of social difference become transformed into "religions" in large part, I would suggest, through discourses of orthodoxy/heresy. Early Christian heresiology, whatever else it is, is largely the work of those who wished to eradicate the fuzziness of the borders, semantic and social, between Jews and Christians and thus produce Judaism and Christianity as fully separate (and opposed) entities—as religions, at least in the eyes of Christianity. (2004, 2)[18]

For Boyarin, then, what constitutes "Jewishness" in late antiquity is not a simple recuperation of a Jewish essence. On the contrary, it is based on a host of social and intellectual forces determined by heresiologists (e.g., early Church fathers, rabbis) who desire to determine fixed boundaries on fluid movements. The danger, according to Boyarin, is that we now assume these borderlines to be firm and grounded in the natural world as opposed to doing social and intellectual work for those who manufactured them in the first place.

Conclusions

This chapter has explored five individuals who have been central in situating Judaism within the academic study of religion in the twentieth century. It is certainly difficult to generalize from their radically different approaches to the material other than, perhaps, to say that they all examined similar data, that produced in the early centuries after the destruction of the Second Temple in 70 CE. None, moreover, were particularly apologetical in the sense that the two non-Jews examined here (Moore and Goodenough) did *not* subscribe to a supersessionist hermeneutic. And the Jews examined here, with the possible exception of Jastrow, were not particularly interested in drawing fences around their data to protect it from analysis. In fact, these case studies show the opposite of what we might expect: that part of the history of studying Jewish data, at least in the American academy, has been one of increasing sophistication using a hermeneutic of suspicion that these texts cannot and must not be taken at face value.

Despite the largely apologetical agendas witnessed in previous chapters, this chapter has revealed the growing integration of Jewish data with some of the theoretical modeling provided by the academic study of religion. This evolving relationship, especially the movement to more critical discourses supplied by the likes of Neusner and Smith (and, of course, D. Boyarin), has the potential to illumine Jewish texts and Jewish communities in ways that are neither apologetic nor descriptive. Whereas so much of the history of writing about Jewish data has implied that Judaism possesses an essence—one that can be neatly differentiated from, say, Christianity (which is then assumed by many to channel the spiritual dimensions of Judaism)—we now see the tendency toward complexity and a greater self-reflection on the very categories used to bring Judaism into existence, to describe rival Judaisms, and the criteria (often extrascholarly) used to differentiate them from other traditions.

This movement is reflective of some of the theoretical developments taking place within departments of religious studies. I do not want to end this chapter with the claim, implicit or otherwise, that all is healthy in this latter discipline and that all that Jewish studies need do is better integrate itself within this larger disciplinary unit. On the contrary, I have tried to call attention to *certain critical trends* within religious studies—trends that query its traditional phenomenological assumptions and that reveal its largely ecumenical and apologetical agenda—and how these can help us look anew at the role and place of Judaism within the academic study of religion.

Before I articulate this potential for integration in greater detail in the final chapter of this study, I switch gears in the following chapter and examine one of the biggest hurdles currently facing the academic study of Judaism.

Private Foundations
Encounter Judaism

As witnessed in chapter 2, the academic study of Judaism began in earnest in Germany during the second half of the nineteenth century. There, a group of young Jews, influenced by the intellectual environment of an academy from which they were ultimately denied teaching positions, began for the first time to apply historical methods to Jewish civilization. Under the guise of historical objectivity and scientific disinterest, they sought to locate Judaism's essence. Despite claims to the contrary, their motivations and objectives were not solely scholarly. Their construction of Judaism was filtered through the prism of rationality and their own desire for political emancipation. They scoured traditional and other sources for that which fit well with their vision: All that coincided with it was signified as "good" and included (e.g., Maimonides and the medieval rationalist tradition), and that which did not was deemed "bad" and excluded (e.g., kabbalah). The result was a highly ideological presentation of what Judaism was and ought to be. Jewish studies has been wrestling with the legacy of these early scholars ever since.[1]

This ideological-charged construction of Judaism, however, is not confined solely to the origins of the field in the nineteenth century. Like any other area or ethnic studies, Jewish studies remains embroiled in issues of representation and authenticity that revolve around issues of identity politics. My concern in this chapter is not the past, but the present. Recent years have witnessed the rise of various private foundations that have the potential to threaten the long-term viability of the academic study of Judaism. These foundations seek inroads into the academy—and presumably the intellectual legitimation that this provides—by establishing various programs, professorships, and conferences in both Jewish studies and Israel studies at North American and Israeli universities.[2] I refer specifically to foundations such as Schusterman, Tikvah, and Posen. All three of these organizations, in their various ways, seek to transform the academic study of Judaism, and all three desire to do so in ways that, perhaps not surprisingly, reflect their own ideological agendas. The unfortunate result is that Jewish studies, rather than liberating itself from its ideological heritage, actually risks reembracing it.

This chapter examines what I consider to be the major dilemma currently facing the modern academic encounter with Judaism. What happens to an academic field once an influx of money with ideological strings attached enters it? Certainly hiring and growth in Jewish studies in this country has always involved the financial support of individual donors. Indeed, as witnessed in chapter 3, Jewish studies would not be where it is today without such munificence. But the rise in recent years of "mega" foundations, such as the aforementioned, is something new and dangerous. These foundations do not simply want to support Jewish studies or Israel studies; they want to transform them and change them from within based on their own understanding of what Judaism is or should be.

If previous chapters have focused on the role of identity and authenticity in scholarship about Judaism over the past century and a half, the present chapter shows how this intersection still operates in the present. As we have seen time and again in this study, the major way that the study of Jewish topics—other than the Old Testament—entered the American university curriculum was through community largesse. This support was never completely disinterested, but—as we have seen—a reflection of community concerns at particular times in the latter's development and functioned as a response to exclusion and anti-Semitism. This has meant that identity politics has always played a role in Jewish studies, as revealed in the controversy that erupted at Queens College when Thomas Bird, a non-Jew, was appointed director of the Jewish Studies Program. Jewish studies, in other words, has a history of wealthy benefactors who endow professorships or even entire programs. This still goes on in the present, but my concern is less with the generosity of private individuals than with multimillion-dollar agencies or foundations that have now begun to fund the academic study of Judaism. These foundations, unlike individuals, have both the organizational and the political wherewithal to translate their vision into action because of both their hands-on approach and the sheer extent of their financial support. In the past such foundations have largely remained on the sidelines—funding and publishing their own journals, engaging in political lobbying, and so on—and only rarely tried to engage or influence academic study.

Now, however, these private and often very wealthy foundations—some of which have very firm ideas of what Judaism is and what "Jewish ideals and values" consist of—can essentially fund and maintain centers at major universities (e.g., Princeton, NYU). This threatens both the autonomy and the viability of the study of Judaism because such centers no longer remain at arm's length from the university, but are now firmly entrenched within its administrative structures. These foundations, then, blur traditional lines between scholarship and politics by the way they fund positions, conferences, book series (at major university presses), journals, and so on.[3]

The result is that the identity politics and the rhetoric of authenticity encountered in previous chapters remain at the center of the field. Whether these politics stress conservative or liberal agendas, based on their own religious or secular politics, such foundations contend that there is something essential to Judaism and that this essence is somehow responsible for the generation of Jewish ideas and values. Such approaches, however, are circular in that the defining essence of Judaism is seen as conforming to the ideological agenda of the foundation in question and then this is subsequently retrofitted onto the historical record. In this respect, there is very little difference between these foundations and the earliest generation of scholars associated with Wissenschaft des Judentums.

A brief survey of some of these organizations will ideally provide a window onto the problems facing Jewish studies within the contemporary university. My goal in surveying these three foundations is not to accuse those who accept their money (through fellowships, conference travel, and so on), but to try to show that the agendas of such foundations—even though the foundations in question may well deny it—seek to transcribe their vision into an academic register and, in the process, influence how Judaism is situated academically.

Charles and Lynn Schusterman Family Foundation

Based in Tulsa, Oklahoma, the Charles and Lynn Schusterman Family Foundation (CLSFF) describes as its overarching goal the desire to ensure "vibrant Jewish life by empowering young Jews to embrace the joy of Judaism, build inclusive Jewish communities, support the State of Israel and repair the world." To accomplish these goals, the CLSFF has, among other things, helped to create and fund the Schusterman Center for Israel Studies at Brandeis University in 2007,[4] in addition to supporting various postdoctoral positions in Israel studies at institutions such as New York University.[5] At first glance, then, the CLSFF alerts us to the fact that one of its central missions is to "support the State of Israel"—but note that nowhere do we learn what this "support" consists of. This support, whatever it may be, is making inroads to the university through the funding of, among other things, positions that deal directly with Israel, one of the most delicate issues in the modern academy. This is clearly not disinterested stuff.

I do not want this argument to be sidetracked by whether support for Israel is good or bad, or what constitutes "good" or "bad" support. If we were to replace "support for Israel" with "support for Palestine" or "support for the Palestinians," we would probably feel quite differently. My point is that once we let wealthy, private institutions into our universities to finance postdoctorates, positions, and programs—let these private institutions essentially fund and dictate what area or ethnic studies should be—we set a dangerous precedent.

Further proof, if indeed such proof is needed, is the CLSFF's involvement in the American-Israel Cooperative Enterprise, a "program that places approximately 20 [Israeli] scholars annually at various U.S. universities." Its Executive Director is Mitchell G. Bard, former editor of the *Near East Report*, the weekly newsletter published by AIPAC, the largest pro-Israel lobby in the United States. The American-Israel Cooperative Enterprise seems to have taken off in light of a controversy that erupted at the University of California, Berkeley, when the post-Zionist[6] Oren Yiftachel was appointed as the first Diller Visiting Professor of Israel Studies in 2004. The so-called "Yiftachel incident" sounded warning bells for all Jewish donors eager to establish a pro-Israeli presence on American campuses. The American-Israel Cooperative Committee Enterprise, in other words, ensures that Israeli scholars of Israel studies are properly vetted and not overly or overtly critical of Zionism. Whereas the left-leaning faculty at UC Berkeley appointed Yiftachel, the American-Israel Cooperative Enterprise insures that candidates are hand chosen by them and only then placed in universities.

In addition to its work in Israel studies, the CLSFF supports the Jewish Studies Expansion Program (JSEP) run by the Foundation for Jewish Culture. The goal of this program is to provide "greater opportunities for Jewish learning and engagement at schools with small and under-resourced Jewish studies programs and keen support from undergraduates, faculty, and administration. A JSEP matching grant permits the hire of a two-year postdoctoral teaching fellow who expands the number of courses offered and helps raise the profile of Jewish studies through cultural programs and other campus activities."[7] The JSEP, then, helps to expand existing programs in Jewish studies by, among other things, funding postdoctorates. Despite this, however, it will only do this at colleges and universities with "relatively large Jewish student populations," a number which it calculates as between "300–1500 Jewish undergraduates."[8] On the Foundation for Jewish Culture website, for example, we read, "The Jewish Studies Expansion Program (JSEP) was established in 2008 in response to significant data that showed Jewish studies courses to have the potential to attract students who might not otherwise engage in Jewish life on campus. JSEP creates more opportunities for Jewish learning and engagement at universities that have relatively large Jewish student populations but only limited ability to offer Jewish studies courses and related extracurricular activities."[9] As this description makes clear, the goal behind the JSEP is not academic, but existential. It desires to use academic programs to make Jewish students more Jewish and, in the process, presumably better "supporters for Israel." Once again we see private monies given to universities, many of which are frequently in need of money owing to the recent economic downturn, with ideological strings attached. I am not even sure if the programs, colleges, and universities that accept this money are aware of these agendas that drive the donations in the first place.

For the sake of both clarity and fairness: I certainly have no intention of diminishing the academic credentials of the young scholars who receive these postdoctorates, and I am certain that they do not all share a monolithic position on Israel. Indeed, many of them have gone on to and will continue to go on to make important contributions to the academic study of Judaism and, hopefully, to their larger disciplinary homes. It is also worth noting that these young scholars are neither appointed nor chosen by the foundations, but hired by academic departments in the universities that have applied for and received a Schusterman Teaching Fellowship. Finally, even though the patronage is aimed at increasing an active Jewish life on campus, many non-Jews certainly also benefit from the increased offerings of classes devoted to Judaism.

I have no quarrel with any of this. My sole concern is that the academic study of Jews and Judaism—something that has really thrived in recent years and that is seeing more and more interest from non-Jewish academics (if, indeed, this is the way one marks "thriving" in the world of Jewish studies)—is potentially being used by a host of wealthy foundations that desire both to impose and to legitimate their particular ideologies.

I mention the CLSFF and the Foundation for Jewish Culture to accentuate the fact that this sort of patronage does not go on, so far as I am aware, for other religious groups on campus. Indeed, we might well chafe if we were to learn that there was a Muslim organization committed to getting young Muslims to engage Islam and Islamic values more actively on campus by funding positions in Islam within departments of religious studies on campuses with relatively large numbers of Muslim students. And whenever Saudis or other wealthy Gulf emirates try to do this, Jewish and other groups keep vigilant eyes on the process.

A good example of this plays out in an earlier iteration of this chapter. I had submitted a version of it to *Zeek*, an online "Jewish journal of thought and culture."[10] Its webpage describes *Zeek* as "an independent magazine. Because we are independent, Zeek is able–and unafraid–to face the most challenging problems in the Jewish world head on."[11] Despite its claim of independence, the editor at the time informed me that he could not publish my "brave" piece because the CLSFF supported another one of his organizations, and he was worried that they might be offended. This is odd because the year before, *Zeek* had published an article highly critical of the Tikvah foundation (Braiterman 2011). The implication is that it was okay for *Zeek* to publish a liberal critique of a conservative organization (Tikvah), but not a similar critique for either a liberal organization (Posen) or one that funds one's own projects (CLSFF).

It would seem, then, that the results of the Schusterman Teaching Fellows on campus benefit all parties involved—Jewish students, non-Jewish students, in addition to academic departments and administrators who do not have to pay for these positions. However, the fact that the Schusterman Family Foundation lists one of its major goals as "support for the State of Israel," the potential for politics and ideology to enter into these positions is omnipresent. What does "support" for the State of Israel mean? Does it mean that one must offer one's support and defend Israel's policies at all costs? Does it mean that one may be critical of certain of Israel's policies (e.g., its refusal to dismantle settlements in the West Bank)? Or, then again, whose Israel is one required to support—the right-wing version of Benjamin Netanyahu or Avigdor Lieberman[12] or the more liberal version of those calling for a fair and just solution the conflict in Israel/Palestine?

Israel—and its defense—is an omnipresent feature in contemporary Jewish studies. In 2006, Alvin Rosenfeld wrote a treatise entitled *"Progressive" Jewish Thought and the New Anti-Semitism* (2006), which was published by the American Jewish Committee,[13] one of the oldest Jewish advocacy organizations in the United States. In his treatise, Rosenfeld set out to answer the following question: "In what ways might Jews themselves, especially so-called 'progressive' Jews, be contributing to the intellectual and political climate that helps to foster such hostility, especially in its anti-Zionist forms?" (Rosenfeld 2006, 1). For Rosenfeld, liberal, what he calls "progressive" (his quotation marks) Jews—especially liberal Jewish academics—pose a danger to the State of Israel. The anti-Israel attitudes of such individuals—and he mentions names such as Daniel Boyarin, Norman Finkelstein, Marc Ellis, and Noam Chomsky—employ "leftist rhetoric" to critique Israeli treatment of Palestinians. This rhetoric and the ways in which it is invoked to describe Israel, he claims, are "indistinguishable from the despised country regularly denounced by the most impassioned anti-Semites" (2006, 20). The goal of these "progressive" Jews, according to Rosenfeld, "is not just to force the Israelis out of the territories they have occupied since 1967, but to force an end to the Jewish state itself" (2006, 20). A critique of Israel's actions in the West Bank, for Rosenfeld, is tantamount to sedition, and when such critiques come from "progressive" academics, it is treasonous.[14]

These are harsh words. They are no less harsh, however, than some of the rhetoric that Rosenfeld seeks to critique in his booklet. My goal is not to choose sides in this high-stakes debate; however, it is to raise awareness of some of the issues involved in both teaching and talking about Jews and Judaism on the contemporary American campus. This can become even more complicated when there are other forces on campus—for example, Muslim Student Associations or Palestinian Student Associations—that regularly engage in anti-Israel activity (such as Israeli Apartheid Week).

Not every "progressive" Jewish academic, however, who is critical of *certain* policies of the State of Israel is tantamount to an anti-Semite (a "self-hating Jew") or to providing fuel for anti-Semitism. Yet, it is a far cry to move from this to conclude, as Rosenfeld does, that calls for "the elimination of the Jewish state—every anti-Semite's cherished dream—are contributed by Jews themselves. Given the drift of 'progressive' Jewish thought, that, too—perverse as it is—should come as no surprise" (2006, 28). Furthermore, I am not sure what the alternative is. Must every Jewish studies faculty member—again we witness the intersection of identity, scholarship, and authenticity—subscribe to a set of positions that defend the State of Israel *at any cost*?

If Jewish studies faculty enter into these discussions about the State of Israel, and it is pretty difficult to avoid them, then the entire Jewish tradition risks being filtered through the prism of the contemporary Israeli-Palestinian conflict.[15] While the position of someone like Rosenfeld, a scholar of the Holocaust, might be formed by the study of anti-Semitism or even the anti-Semitic portrayal of Judaism in the

American academy as surveyed in the previous chapter, his portrayal of those Jewish academics who are critical of certain Israeli policies as facilitators of anti-Semitism is problematic.

In this section we have seen how private Jewish institutions (e.g., the Charles and Lynn Schusterman Family Foundation, the American Jewish Committee) are intimately involved with the situation of Judaism within the modern university. Whereas the Schusterman Foundation seeks to help small Jewish studies programs with relatively large numbers of Jewish students increase its course offerings with the aim of getting such students involved in Jewish life on campus and presumably making them better supporters of Israel, the American Jewish Committee publishes works that seeks to "out" liberal Jewish studies academics. The result is that—and this should certainly not come as any surprise given what we have seen in the past four chapters—the academic study of Judaism is intimately intertwined with a set of larger features that concern the fate of something collectively referred to as "the Jewish people."

Tikvah Fund

The late Zalman Bernstein (1926–1999), a venture capitalist and ardent Zionist, founded the Tikvah Fund with the "hope that by investing in great Jewish ideas and Jewish leaders, the heritage he cherished and the people he loved would be a light unto all nations."[16] Central to his and the Fund's goal is the elucidation of something that they refer to as "Jewish ideas" and how such ideas can function in the political governance of the modern State of Israel, something that presumably has the ability to make it "a light unto the nations." The result, however, is ultimately a neoconservative Jewish reading of the "great books" of the Western political-philosophical tradition to uphold a particular form of Zionism.

The problem with Tikvah, as it will be for its more liberal cousin, Posen, is that there is an assumption that ideas exist in the world and that they can be neatly reified as "Jewish" (or "Western" or "Islamic"). In their desire to construct a particular identity, both Tikvah and Posen ignore cultural and intellectual fluidity. Jewish identity, like any identity, is imagined and constructed in light of a host of internal and external stimuli. For the Tikvah and Posen foundations, however, there is no interest in this identity maintenance because it contradicts their desire to find the essence of Jewish peoplehood and the ideas that they believe are responsible for sustaining it.

The Tikvah Fund's mission statement, reflecting the goals of its founder, is simple and presumably innocuous enough:

> The mission of the Tikvah Fund is to promote serious Jewish thought about the enduring questions of human life and the pressing challenges that confront the Jewish people. Tikvah will support many programs, projects, and individuals—including new university centers and courses, books and journals, summer seminars and scholarships. Tikvah's work will be grounded in these fundamental convictions: that the great ideas, texts, and traditions of Judaism are a special inheritance, with much to teach everyone in search of wisdom about the human condition; and that the fate of the Jewish people greatly depends on the education of intellectual, religious, and political leaders, both in Israel and the Diaspora.[17]

In itself, there is certainly nothing the matter with such a mission—the study of "serious" Jewish thought would, in theory, seem to be something positive. Who would not want to study traditional Jewish sources "seriously"? The problem, however, is that upon closer scrutiny, we find out that Tikvah's board of directors is overwhelmingly neo-conservative (e.g., Roger Hertog, Neal Kozodoy, Eric Cohen, William Kristol). A board that is so overwhelmingly committed to a particular political ideology means that we should probably go back and examine words in the previous quotation such as "support," "fundamental convictions," and even question what "serious Jewish thought" might mean for such individuals.

A perfect example is the Tikvah-sponsored Shalem Center in Israel. Founded in 1994, its goal is to create the first liberal arts college in Israel. (Its webpage lists fellow neocon Martin Kramer as its president-delegate.)[18] A quick perusal of their literature and a glance at their patrons and board of directors, who also play a key role in the Tikvah Fund, and it soon becomes clear that their goal is more than just setting up a liberal arts college. Its first president, Yoram Hazony—a close friend and confidant of hawkish Israeli prime minister, Benjamin Netanyahu—put right-wing politicians such as Natan Sharansky and Moshe Ya'alon on its staff (Lanski and Berman 2007). Sharansky, for example, was the director of the Sheldon Adelson-funded Institute for Strategic Studies at Shalem.[19]

If it were just a matter of having rightwing and neocons on their board of directors things might be otherwise. However, the views of

such individuals are at the heart of the Shalem Center and its fledgling college. Its current president, Daniel Polisar, for example, writes
of the Jewish people:

> Over more than three millennia, the Jewish people achieved
> extraordinary longevity and success on the strength of ideas.
> From the time of the Bible, the Jews advanced concepts that
> transformed the world, including the dignity of man, the
> unity of God, the sanctity of law, and the desirability of
> a political order based on sovereign national states living
> together in peace. These ideas have united Jews around a
> common set of beliefs, given them courage to hold fast to
> their convictions in the face of opposition and persecution,
> and enabled them to influence decisively the philosophy
> and history of much of humankind.[20]

Here Polisar uses a trope that we have seen frequently in this study,
that of the "gift of the Jews." We encountered this in chapter 1 when
I examined, for example, the work by David Gelernter, something
that, it should come as no surprise now, the Tikvah Fund underwrote.
According to Polisar (and Gelernter), Jews are responsible for creating
some of the ideas central to Western civilization—monotheism, ethics,
"sovereign nation states living together in peace." He also emphasizes
how these ideas have "united" Jews throughout the millennia. This
unity is important because, as he will argue subsequently, one of
the greatest threats to the Jews today is both anti-Semitism directed
from without *and* internal division. The latter presumably refers to all
those Jews who disagree with the conservative mandate of the Shalem
Center and the larger Tikvah Fund, of which it is a part (a group not
unlike Rosenfeld's "Progressive" Jews). In the paragraph subsequent
to the one mentioned above, Polisar goes on to talk about current
dangers: "But the challenges facing Israel and the Jewish people did
not end with the establishment of a sovereign state. Indeed, while
Jews today face unparalleled opportunities for a cultural renaissance
that could also benefit not only the West but world civilization more
generally, they also face enormous dangers from assimilation and disunity from within, and resurgent anti-Semitism and strategic threats
to Israel from without" (ibid.).

   This talk of assimilation and disunity is problematic. How does
he define "assimilation"? Surely some of the best ideas produced by
Jews have occurred when they have lived within and partaken of
other cultures. Or does he mean intermarriage, always a trump card

pulled out in support of various ideological battles within the Jewish world? Similarly, what does he mean by "disunity"? This, once again, seems to be a return to Rosenfeld's position that was directed to those whom he pejoratively labeled as "progressive" Jews. It seems that those Jews who do not want to see anti-Semitism around every corner or that disagree with some of the State of Israel's policies toward the Palestinians or its Arab neighbors create "disunity" among the Jewish people. Polisar goes on to state that the solution to anti-Semitism and internal disunity comes from "ideas":

> The response must come, first of all, in the realm of ideas. It is crucial to develop an understanding of Jewish thought and tradition that can serve as the basis for unity in Israel and throughout the Jewish world; create an understanding of Jewish and Zionist history that instills pride and solidarity while maintaining fidelity to the highest standards of scholarship; harness the Jewish and Western political traditions to provide a firm basis for steering Israel as a democracy and a Jewish national state; craft a diplomatic and military strategy that will ensure Israel's survival in an increasingly hostile world; and develop economic and social policies that will enable Israel to be a prosperous and just society. (Ibid.)

Once again, we witness the intersection of the study of Judaism and the need for "instilling pride and solidarity." Recall that one of the major goals behind the origins of Wissenschaft des Judentums discussed in chapter 2 was to show Jews that they, too, possessed a history and that an appreciation of this would show them that they were just like the other nations of Europe. At the Shalem Center, Polisar and his staff have tried to create a curriculum that uses the classics of Western political theory—the "great books" that are now interpreted from a conservative Jewish and Zionist perspective—in order to legitimate their own particular understanding of Judaism, of Zionism, and of Jewish peoplehood.

The Tikvah Foundation also sponsors numerous programs in North America. These include the Tikvah Center for Jewish Law and Civilization at NYU and the Tikvah Project on Jewish Thought at Princeton University. Both of these centers, not unlike the Shalem Center, are interested in Jewish contributions to Western civilization—law in the case of NYU, and philosophy in the case of Princeton—and in how Western canons of law and philosophy can help universalize those of Judaism. Both centers fund seminars, and publish books and journals. The Tikvah Fund is also the major backer of a popular journal devoted to "Jewish ideas," *The Jewish Review of Books* (for a critique of this, see Braiterman 2011).

The problem with the Tikvah Fund, in all of its many iterations, is that it reifies Jewish ideas. It assumes that ideas develop in hermetically sealed cultural vacuums. It has no problems determining that something is "Jewish" or something is "Western"—both of which can be signified positively—or when something is "Arab" or "Islamic," which can be signified pejoratively. The Tikvah Fund, including all of the projects it supports, is unwilling or unable to envisage the cross-pollination of cultures. Instead it subscribes to an essentialist vision of what Judaism is—monotheistic, democratic, Zionist.

The Posen Foundation

Felix Posen, an English philanthropist who made his money in the oil, metal, minerals, and coal business, is an individual deeply committed both to the secular study of Judaism and to anti-Semitism. In support of the latter, the Posen Foundation is the primary benefactor of the Vidal Sassoon International Center for the Study of Anti-Semitism at the Hebrew University of Jerusalem.[21] The foundation is also behind the Felix Posen Bibliographic Project, which is dedicated to listing every book, journal article, and scholarly treatise on the subject of anti-Semitism written in any language and published anywhere in the world; this is in addition to the Posen Papers in Contemporary anti-Semitism, which, according to the description on its website, aims "to provide a rapid response and immediate orientation in the present wave of global anti-Semitism."[22]

On top of its funding and supporting original work on the study of anti-Semitism, the Posen Foundation provides financial incentives to faculty members to create courses and conferences on cultural Judaism, that is, a Judaism that is not interested in either a theological presentation or in data that is imagined as religious (e.g., rabbinic texts). If the goal of the Tikvah Fund is to create and disseminate a politically neoconservative and religiously Orthodox interpretation of Judaism, the Posen Foundation sees as its mandate the dissemination of a more liberal and secular vision. To quote from its webpage:

> The Posen Foundation works internationally as a service
> provider to support secular Jewish education and educa-

tional initiatives on Jewish culture in the modern period and the process of Jewish secularization over the past three centuries. At a time when the majority of world Jewry defines itself as secular and is not well educated in Jewish culture, the Foundation offers this growing community the opportunity to deepen and enrich the study of its cultural and historic heritage—from a secular, scholarly perspective.[23]

To ensure this "secular, scholarly perspective," the Posen Foundation is committed to any project that will further its agenda. It supports seminars and conferences, funds endowed professorships on cultural and secular Judaism at various universities, and it is in the process of creating the Posen Library of Jewish Culture and Civilization (Yale University Press).[24] Its most popular program, however, is that which funds academic courses on secular Judaism. "Each institution" that receives such a grant, to quote from its webpage, "has received development grants between $35,000 to $50,000 per year for three years through the Posen Project."[25] The description of this program ensures that the Posen vision of Judaism is taught: "The Program funds the development and implementation of one or more 'core courses' in the history of secular Jewish thought and/or culture. These courses in Jewish thought, history, sociology, anthropology, or other related disciplines—or ideally an interdisciplinary course—examine the process of Jewish secularization over the past three centuries or focus specifically and explicitly on the secular traditions within modernity."[26] This program ensures that Posen's vision is disseminated on campuses throughout North America and Israel. According to its website, since 2003, "the Foundation has funded courses at 40 universities in North America, Israel, and Europe involving more than 100 academics and 1500 students." This essentially amounts to the Tikvah Fund, but from across the ideological divide.

The Posen Foundation also supports the publication of books. A prime example of the latter is David Biale's *Not in the Heavens: The Tradition of Jewish Secular Thought* published by Princeton University Press in 2011. In the preface, Biale thanks Felix Posen, whose foundation provided him with "a year of uninterrupted research and writing away from my usual academic duties" (xiii). He also calls Posen "that rarest of philanthropists who takes deep intellectual interest in the causes he supports" and whose vision has had "an enormously stimulating effect on a generation of Jewish Studies scholars" (xiii).

In his opening chapter, Biale has a section entitled "Precursors," wherein he examines in seven short pages all of, what are to him at least, the "precursors" to Jewish atheism and secularism that begin in earnest with Spinoza in the seventeenth century. On his reading, for example, one begins to find even as early as biblical writings in the Second Temple period "a thoroughgoing skepticism about the God of History" (2011, 16). God's perceived absence, writes Biale, led to the development of new genres, of which the book of Esther must be included, for this book "is first and foremost a tale of politics in the Diaspora, and its lessons are thoroughly secular" (17). I have no idea how Biale can try to separate the "political," "religious," and "secular" in the fourth or third century BCE.

In the same "Precursor" section, Biale next turns his attention to Maimonides and the medieval rationalist tradition as unconscious precursors to secularism. Although Biale does not worry about the intricacies of Maimonides' highly complex thought ("[it] is complex and need not detain us here"), he has no qualms about showing how it "could" lead to the type of "atheism" found in Spinoza: "Although Maimonides holds that a chain of negation leads ultimately to the affirmation of God's unity (albeit in the form of a negative proposition), it could just as well—against Maimonides' intentions—lead to the final, big negation of atheism: a God so transcendent that "he" cannot be described is virtually a God that doesn't exist" (2011, 20). Biale is certainly not interested in the thought of Maimonides here. If he were, he would spend considerable time on the Aristotelian and the medieval Islamic tradition that contributed to Maimonides' conception of negative attributes of God. Instead we witness a particular revisionist reading in which Maimonides (against his own intentions, no less) "could" lead to atheism. Maimonides, however, was not an atheist, nor was he a secularist or even a protosecularist. In fact, his thought is nothing like Spinoza's. However, in Biale's narrative it has to be because he wants to show how "Spinoza's revolution had its feet firmly planted in the Middle Ages" (2011, 22).

Posen's revisionism, much like the revisionism of Tikvah, is that it again reaffirms that the vision of something called "Jewish" history is entirely internal. There is little recognition of external cultural and historical influences—the ancient Near East in the case of the Bible, the Arabo-Islamic intellectual traditions in the Middle Ages—only much talk about "protosecular" Judaism that occurs in a vacuum and is completely decontextualized from the intellectual milieux in which Jews lived.

The Posen Foundation is also currently in the process of creating, as mentioned, a projected ten-volume "Posen Library of Jewish Culture and Civilization." In its desire to see only "secular" or "cultural" Judaism, however, the Posen Foundation not only excises that which does not conform to its definition of secularism (for example, I see no projects devoted therein to any Jewish topic prior to Spinoza), but it also makes a monolith out of that type of Judaism that it has created in its own image—for example, that there are such things in the world as secular "Jewish" values or ideals. Moreover, it seems to conflate "Jewish secularism" with the secular study of Jewish texts, as if the latter cannot take place without the former.

In its goals, the Posen Foundation is certainly no different than either Schusterman or Tikvah. Like them, Posen seeks to find *the* Jewish essence, one not surprisingly that conforms to its own image, and one that can function as the catalyst to renew modern Jewish identity from within. This identity, however, is never seen as constructed or imagined, but always as eternal and essential. And it is in precisely this regard that we are taken back to the early years of Wissenschaft des Judentums—where a generation of scholars sought to define the essence of Judaism, in a highly ideologically charged fashion, for political gain.

Conclusions

The danger of such organizations is that their forays into the academy are based on ideology. Will some scholars who receive grants from these foundations do good work and put the money to good use? Certainly. I have no doubt that most do innovative things with such grants. The issue for me, however, is not those who receive the grants, but that we—whoever we are (university administrators in need of private donations, ideologues who agree with their visions, faculty in search of a semester at Princeton or NYU)—have allowed foundations that are based on one particular vision of what Judaism is or should be to operate within the administrative structures of university campuses. None of these foundations, despite appeals to the contrary, is interested in funding scholarship simply for its own sake. It would seem, though all would deny it, that to be eligible for funding from any of these sources one must share, *to some degree*, the vision of the foundation. I certainly do not want to claim that everyone who receives a fellowship from the Tikvah is a neoconservative Zionist or that everyone who receives support from the Posen Foundation is a liberal Jew who is only interested in secular trends since the time of Mendelssohn. However, it is important to note that, no matter how these foundations disperse their monies, they stand for something, and they have a particular ideological slant. And this is not necessarily good for the general health of the field.

Although my own intellectual leanings may well come closer to that of Posen, I mistrust any private foundation that seeks to entrench itself in the academy with promises of conference travel, publication subvention, and money to develop courses. At a time when university funds are shrinking, the infiltration of private foundations—no matter what the ideological stripe—into the university sets a dangerous precedent. All private monies in the university come with strings attached. The university curriculum, with its theoretical commitment to objectivity and disinterest, is not the place for wealthy private foundations that desire academic legitimation.

I tried to make the case at the beginning of this chapter that these wealthy, private foundations are regressive, taking the field of Jewish studies back to another time, to its origins. Jewish studies began in a highly politicized and ideologically charged environment as scholars, associated with the various denominations of Judaism, created a series of Judaisms in their own images. All privileged and denied certain aspects of the tradition in the service of some larger ideological project. In many ways, given the politics of the day, it could not have been otherwise. However, rather than interrogate their presuppositions, showing their unchecked assumptions, many seem content to carry on in the same path, accepting money that comes from organizations with their own assumption of what Judaism is.

On one level, these foundations carry on a project that we have seen throughout this work, namely, the private support behind the academic study of Judaism. Without private monies, Jewish studies would never have entered the university curriculum. The great paradox, of course, is that private money has largely ensured that Jewish studies has become what it is today: a vibrant and interdisciplinary academic enterprise. However, behind such private money resides the potential threat of control and ideology. It is because of this latter aspect that we should be cautious of the various foundations examined in this chapter. An examination of their boards of directors, the language of their mission statements, how they construct Judaisms based on a series of privilege and denial all clearly reveal that these foundations are not interested in supporting Jewish studies for the sake of disinterested scholarship.

I think we—Jewish studies scholars at the present moment—must be vigilant. I certainly would not want to see these foundations completely disappear. However, I do think they ought to be kept at arm's length and that they ought to be honest about what they are doing. When they are the ones funding our academic programs, there will be a price to pay. I once had a colleague say to me, in jest, that we have a choice now: Posen *or* Tikvah. In an ideal world, it should be *neither* Posen *nor* Tikvah.

6

Future Prospects

In this last chapter, I would like to move from Jewish studies' past to its future, from what was to what might well be. The history of Jewish studies—caught up in the desire for emancipation, inclusion, and normalization—has left its indelible mark on the present. The previous five chapters have tried to understand and contextualize these desires, showing how they still play a large role in how Judaism is imagined and encountered within the ebb and flow of other disciplinary contexts. Jewish studies is perennially caught, as witnessed time and again in the previous pages, between the forces of particularism and universalism, between ethnic studies with its emphasis on insularity, and disciplinarity that, at least in theory, is not interested in issues of special pleading. Jewish studies' present must look to its past in order to redress certain of its more apologetic features for its future vitality.

If the past has largely been defined by the desire for recognition and inclusion into the mainstream university curriculum, its future must be one of increased interdisciplinary relevance based on the twin principles of extroversion and autonomy. The former means the acknowledgment that Jewish data is neither unique nor special, but constructed and contested in the same manner that any other dataset is. The latter means that it is necessary to counter the rise of private foundations that seek to shape the field based on various ideological agendas. Within this latter context, the previous chapter recounted one possible future, one wherein such foundations determine what counts as "Jewish" (and even what gets to count as "Jewish studies") and what does not. In times of economic instability and the increasing diminishment of university resources, the financial largesse of such foundations set, simultaneously, a financially attractive yet very dangerous precedent. This situation, I argued, reveals the parallels between past and present and their repercussions for the future. Replicating both the insularity of Wissenschaft des Judentums and the role of outside money in the development of Jewish studies, such foundations risk making scholarship beholden to a set of interests that are decidedly nonscholarly.

This meddling—and it is certainly not unique to Jewish studies[1]—undermines the entire foundation upon which scholarship is at least in theory based. Even though the beginnings of Jewish studies may well have been in apologetics and pleas for Jewish inclusion, it need not end in an introspective agenda that refuses to acknowledge the fluid boundaries between what is "Jewish" and what is "non-Jewish," a refusal grounded as it is in larger ideological frameworks that seek to use scholarship for their own uses and abuses. Instead, it becomes necessary for the academic study of Judaism to disengage from the financial support of such ideologues. The future, in other words, must be open to a set of *mutually beneficial* conversations with other humanities disciplines.[2] The insularity and introspection of Jewish studies can be laid neither solely nor simply at the door of Jewish studies, however. Here, it is important to keep in mind the history of Jewish exclusion both in Germany in the nineteenth century and in America during much of the first two-thirds of the twentieth century. Despite the fact that it was largely self-financed in this country for much of its history, Jewish studies was able to flourish largely on account of its academic integrity based as it was on the ability to keep private monies and academic pursuits separate from one another.

Now, however, the forces for exclusion are centripetal, not centrifugal. There is a tendency to encounter Judaism—in addition to constructing it as responsible for all that is good in the West (e.g., its "moral and spiritual direction," to quote David Gelernter)—as if it existed in isolation and then appreciating and understanding it as somehow ontologically or taxonomically distinct from other cultural and/or religious forms. Rather than be integrated into the university curriculum, Jewish studies is now potentially conceived as standing apart, as somehow unique, by those who engage in its study. The result is that we have almost come full circle: whereas in the beginnings of Jewish studies, non-Jews sought to keep the study of Judaism (with the exception of ancient Israel and its spiritual fulfillment in Jesus) in Jewish seminaries, we now witness the study of Jewish data—self-constructed as sui generis—in self-imposed departments or centers that function as quasiseminaries.

The question that Jewish studies must answer as it faces the future, a question that is common to all area or ethnic studies programs, is how to reconcile with the larger interests or questions of the humanities and the social sciences. The remainder of this chapter will explore these tensions and their potential resolution in greater detail. What, given the major disciplinary focus of this study, can Jewish studies learn from the academic study of religion? What, in turn, can religious studies learn from the academic study of Judaism? Now is certainly the time to begin the process of putting together these two academic disciplines in a manner that they can potentially cross-pollinate with one another.

In what follows, I turn to this process of reconciliation. In so doing, I stress points of contact between the academic studies of Judaism and religion that revolve around issues of critical theory in the context of the latter discipline. I refer particularly to a set of discourses that are primarily interested in demonstrating the constructed and ideological nature of the terms and categories that we use to conjure our data into existence. It is these terms and categories, their implicit assumptions and rhetorical moves, that we need to query with an eye toward how it is that we create taxonomies and other models, and for what purposes we engage in such purposes in the first place.

Judaism on the Margins

It is important to resist the temptation to assume that communities simply constitute themselves around a set of essential qualities. Judaism for so much of its development was in conversation with—both defining itself and being defined by—rival religious traditions (e.g., various forms of Christianities and Islams). The lines, although often perceived as ontological or taxonomic, that separated Judaism from these other religions were neither firm nor fixed; rather, they were fluid, as ideas and social patterns moved freely, anonymously, and often unnoticed across them. One of the great perils in the academic study of Judaism (or any other religion) is the assumption that in the world there naturally exists something "Jewish," that which is somehow imagined as essentially different from other "religions," and then placing this marker or signifier onto earlier times and different places. The tendency that assumes religious identities neatly and effortlessly move, Geist-like, across or through the historical record must, in other words, be resisted.

If the critical discourses in religious studies to which I referred above tell us anything, it is that we must not assume the givenness of our categories. "Religion," as I argued in the introduction, is an inherently vague term, one that is largely the product of our own imagining. The term "religion," including its adjective "religious," as others have argued, is a largely Western creation and imposition that is grounded in political hegemony (Fitzgerald 2000; Dubuisson 2003). In addition, by employing it there is a tendency to marginalize a host of political, ideological, economic, and social factors, thereby potentially skewing our understanding of the data in question. To claim that something is "religious," for example, may mean that we overlook the manifold ways that it connects to other human-created and socially constructed factors. The category "religion" obfuscates more than it clarifies.

The same could certainly be said for "Jewish" or "Judaism." Once we reify such terms, we potentially make them into stable entities, ones that admit of seemingly hard boundaries that make it possible to declare nonchalantly what is "in" and what is "out." The moment we do this, however, we give Judaism an essence (e.g., monotheistic, legal, ethical) against which either rival Judaisms or other religions are judged and found wanting. In their desire to create a normative Judaism in their own images, groups such as Tikvah and Posen discussed in the previous chapter build upon this model in their desire to encounter a Judaism that fits with their particular political slant. The criterion for inclusion in such conceptual modeling is the ability to see reflected in certain data one's own image.

One of the major tasks facing the academic study of Judaism at the present moment, it seems to me, is how to curtail the influence of such groups and their desire to define what Judaism is (and fund those who agree with it or who help to bring it into existence). An examination of Judaism at/on the margins, including the complex intersection between center and borders, strikes me as one important way to go about challenging traditional assumptions and their modern iterations. This is certainly not the only reason to stress "border" or "boundary" studies. Indeed, my reason for examining it in this chapter is to show how such study reveals a complex myriad of Judaisms that interact in complex and polyvalent ways with other religious traditions, especially Christianities and Islams. Such interactions reveal sets of mutually overlapping characteristics and criteria in which more of these characteristics are shared between the traditions than not.

Rather than speak about "Judaism" in the way that both tradition and normativity encourage us, it makes much more sense to speak, following the likes of Neusner and Smith encountered in chapter 4, of "Judaisms." But this is not simply a grammatical shift in which a noun in the singular is simply replaced by its plural form. On the contrary, the shift in number needs to be understood to be semantic so that we now acknowledge diversity, conflict, and commotion over rival interpretations of authority based on the rhetoric of authenticity. To employ the singular of any tradition, by contrast, is to create a monolithic entity that, while perhaps appealing to religious sensibilities, does very little to help us understand complexity on the ground. "Judaism," "Christianity," and "Islam" (not to mention other religious traditions) do not represent three discrete essences, but become canopies under which cohabit multiple Judaisms, Christianities, and Islams. Once we acknowledge this, we begin to witness the fixed and often heavily patrolled borders between these three discrete traditions begin to break down and even collapse. On the microlevel, we now encounter subgroups from each of the three religions that begin to resemble one another more closely with respect to particular features than they do to other subgroups within the same religion. It is unfortunate that much of our intellectual energy is expended on what is going on at the macrolevel that we often lose sight of what is happening at the microlevel.[3]

It is, on the contrary, in the overlapping and complex interactions among Judaisms, Christianities, and Islams that we encounter various struggles, skirmishes, and the desire to imagine manifold identity formations. To reduce these complexities to the singular of each tradition is to miss much of how the practices and the identities that both produce and are produced by them are formed, maintained, and later patrolled. Despite the fact that it has increasingly become trendy to use the plural "religions," Russell McCutcheon writes that this has merely shifted the earlier rhetoric, with the use of plurals (e.g., "religions," Judaisms") "now being more acceptable than singulars (as if it is completely sensible to talk about 'dogs' when, again for whatever reason, we no longer use 'dog' to name a distinct biological grouping)" (McCutcheon 2012, 1). The result is real ambivalence in which "things" or "concepts" (e.g., religions, Judaisms) are thought to exist outside of the categories or taxonomies that bring them into existence in the first place.

Too much thinking and the expenditure of too much energy—in religious studies more generally and in Jewish studies in particular—have revolved around trying to articulate religions as if they were discrete units existing naturally in the world instead of heuristic objects of analysis. There is a tendency, in other words, to speak about "*the* Jewish Experience" (or "*the* Muslim experience" or "*the* Buddhist experience") as if it existed as a reified object. My suggestion here is that it now becomes necessary to move beyond taking such terms or experiences as given and instead envisage them for what they are: the ideological products of particular framers (whether in antiquity or in the present) of what they consider to be the authentic expression of Judaism (whether in antiquity or in the present).

Yet, on account of the proximity of Judaisms to other Near Eastern monotheistic traditions, we can catch glimpses of the fluidity of boundaries between them. Rather than obscure these glimpses by using imprecise hermeneutic categories derived from theological or quasitheological agendas that emphasize the monolithic and tidy at the expense of the multiform and complex, we need to rethink our methods of analysis. It is usually assumed, for example, that Judaism, Christianity, and Islam—as discrete religions—simply bumped up alongside one another and exchanged ideas. Judaism produced Christianity in the first century CE, and both gave rise to Islam in the seventh century. Far less attention, however, is given to the dynamics of how, why, when, and by whom such interactions occurred.[4] What, for example, might the formation, maintenance, and dissolution of group identity mean, and how might these processes give rise to the existential and doctrinal dilemmas of negotiating how Jews were both like and unlike, similar and foreign to, Christians, Muslims, and other members of the larger Mediterranean and European worlds they inhabited?

Rather than imagine Judaism as a container with fixed boundaries that is full of something (presumably "Jewishness"), it might be more productive to extend and expand our sense of conceptual modeling. What, to use but one example, are the various "thick" contexts wherein cultural meanings are produced, deployed, and contested? How might the contours between Jews and others look if we move beyond traditional signifiers used to describe their interactions—signifiers such as "tolerance," "intolerance," "heroism," and "victimhood"? What if, in their stead, we use descriptive lenses that switch our focus from fixed identity and its simple recuperation to the task of communal invention and reinvention?

Too much work throughout the length and breadth of Jewish scholarly writing, something I trust most of the previous five chapters have demonstrated in considerable detail, has focused on elucidating "Jewishness" and its various arts of perseverance. As I suggested above, there are real communal and political reasons for doing this—reasons that cannot simply be gainsaid or written off as apologetics, but ones that are grounded in a host of exclusionary and anti-Semitic forces. This has meant that there is a tendency to make "Judaism," and whatever it may mean or however it may be constructed, exist uncomfortably alongside other religions, most specifically Christianity and Islam. The creation of readily and easily identifiable demarcations, predicated as they are on the above model of essences, has become a methodological necessity in Jewish studies.

But what if we switch focus from centers to margins? Taking the lead of scholars such as Bodian (1999), D. Boyarin (2004), J. Boyarin (2008, 2009), and E. Wolfson (e.g., 2010a), the moment we ask new questions of old data we find ourselves on new and uncertain terrain. Reified categories we have long taken for granted—"Jews," "Christians," and "Muslims"—and the various models we have used to account for their interaction—"antagonism," "symbiosis"—no longer hold methodologically. Framed anew, as we have witnessed in previous chapters, they all become freighted with much ideological baggage. All of these terms and the methodologies that both produce and maintain them are ultimately invested in the desire, on the part of scholars (whether rabbinically or academically trained), to maintain the coherence and legitimacy of identity. Rather than show its investment in numerous wills to powers, the tendency of much traditional religious studies scholarship has been to reproduce it, not query it.

With its investments in other monotheisms, Jewish data possesses the *potential* to illumine a great deal. Focusing on boundaries and shared cultural worlds, we see a productive breakdown of traditional paradigms. On this level, rather than use the models that regard essential Judaism, Christianity, and Islam as working with or against one another, it becomes useful to examine specific, localized encounters that involve common cultural vocabularies or semantics around which various subcultures within each of the so-called religions define themselves. Some of these subcultures may well exhibit greater similarities with subcultures of the other two "religions" than they do with those of what we often think of as their own. Many subgroups, whether assimilating to or fighting against such shared cultural semantics, ultimately define group identity in similar ways. This messiness and overlap, however, has often been neatly dismissed, even in academic circles associated with religious studies, using the "orthodox/heterodox" binary. Yet such binaries are usually constructed much later and only imposed retroactively. When we say that this is what "Judaism" looked like in late antiquity or what "Islam" looked like in the eighth century, and so on, we have to ask: for whom and for what purposes?

It is this complex set of similarities, what theorists of yesteryear used to call family resemblances, that most interests me here. Yet I am not interested in these resemblances in a phenomenological or an ahistorical manner. On the contrary, we need to focus on how

subgroups from different religious traditions can often share more
similarities than they do with other subgroups within their own religion. In fact, the very term "religion," and all of the baggage that it
carries in its wake, is probably not even the best term to use. Like so
many of our "analytical" terms, it has the propensity to force square
pegs into round holes for the sake of order.

The question is not what is Judaism, but how is Judaism produced? If the former question implies a center or a certain fixity, the
latter carries in its wake issues of fluidity and active production. Judaism is not something "out there" that various texts (be it the Bible or
the Talmud) elucidate. On the contrary, these texts are sites of contest
that seek to create, establish, and disseminate what is considered to
be authentic Judaism. Although disciplinary norms tell us that such
texts contribute to our understanding of the "religion" of Judaism,
we could just as easily say that such works function as propaganda
grounded in the ideological claims of their authors/redactors.

Judaisms, Christianities, Islams

In this section, I wish to move from a model that envisages antagonism between Judaism and rival monotheisms to one that sees free
exchange and interchange. Based on the, for lack of a better term,
"border discourse" of the previous section, a potentially viable and
healthy future for Jewish studies is one that is not concerned with
essences (e.g., "*what* is Judaism"), but with production (e.g., "*how* is
Judaism imagined and *by whom?*").

Judaism, whether in the second century CE, the seventh century,
or even today, takes place against a backdrop of sectarian, ideological,
and social interests. For example, the partition of "Judeo-Christianity,"
according to Daniel Boyarin, is not something grounded in the natural
order. Contrary to traditional consensus that sees (rabbinic) Judaism
emerge first and then quickly followed by Christianity, each with its
own set of religious forms and practices, Boyarin argues that there
were no such characteristics or features that could be described as
uniquely "Jewish" or "Christian" in the late antique period. Instead,
he argues that Jesus-following Jews and Jews who did not follow
Jesus would have inhabited the same cultural and intellectual space
and would have shared identical practices (e.g., keeping kosher, Sabbath observance). What eventually emerged as two discrete religions
was not based on such practices, but was the result of later heresiologists—Boyarin felicitously refers to them as "border makers"—who

sought to define certain beliefs and practices as "Christian" and others as "Jewish" (i.e., as heretical). In so doing, these later thinkers were responsible for moving ideas, behaviors, and ultimately people, to one side or another of an artificial border. Articulating this complexity, he writes:

> The net result will be that there might indeed be people who are prototypes of *Jew* but are also *Christian* (say a Pharisee who observes all of the Pharisaic laws and rules but believes that Jesus is the Messiah), and moreover, that the "best example" of *Jew* and *Christian* would almost definitely be both a politically charged and a diachronically varying category. Further while there would be Jews who would not recognize certain other Jews as such, there might be ones whom they would recognize as Jews who would recognize in turn those others as Jews, setting up the possibility of chained communion or communication. This would then be an example of a family resemblance with the additional element of agency among members of the family itself. An example of this phenomenon (from the other side) would be Justin who recognizes as Christians precisely those Jewish Christians to whom Jerome, much later of course, would deny the name *Christian*, but Jerome would certainly recognize Justin as Christian. Those so-called Jewish Christians surely thought of themselves as both Jews and Christians, and some non-Christian Jews may have recognized them as Jews as well. (2004, 25–26)

Boyarin here wonderfully sets up the complexity of the situation "on the ground" and how this social complexity and shared cultural space belies tidy attempts to define discrete religious traditions as in place or complete with a set of identity markers to which believers simply subscribe. These markers, on the contrary, are the products of later generations, those who want to create a set of categories to make sense of their social worlds. But categories, as Boyarin well notes, are by nature fuzzy, and, it seems to me, it is precisely this fuzziness of sociocultural division that leads to the desire to make them into ontological signifiers.

The ambiguity of categories, both religious and nonreligious, means that certain individuals—those charged with order and maintenance—desire to transform complexity and opaqueness into a set of neat identity markers with clearly demarcated borders. If you believe or subscribe to "x," for example, you are in, and if you do not believe "x," then you are out. Yet the situation, as Boyarin reminds us here, is much more complex than our so-called primary sources let on. Rather than take such sources as clear, we need to see how they are invested—as any other text—in ideological debates over identity and the social construction of reality. What then do we do with religious texts? Rather than see them as timeless products of the religious imagination, we need to see them as ideologically charged documents. Such texts, on Boyarin's reading, need to be perceived "not as reflective of social realities but as social apparatuses that are understood to be complexly tied to other apparatuses via the notion of a discourse or a *"dispositif"* (2004, 27).

The categories employed by "border makers" now become part of a checklist of features that subsequently determine who is "in" and who is "out" of the group, defining who is self and who other in the process. And although particular power centers (e.g., the Church, rabbinic academies) may be well served by the hardening of these borders, they are also imposed on all others by imperial fiat and "operations of hegemony" (2004, 26). They are, moreover, borders that probably remain much more fluid for longer periods of time than these power centers let on. If we take these early heresiologists, of which Church fathers or rabbinic authorities function as a subset, as heavily invested in the creation and maintenance of borders, then hopefully we begin to see how invested they are in not just establishing identity, but also in actively creating it.

Boyarin's analysis shows us the dangers of positing that to each religion there is an essence or set of essences that neatly differentiate it from others. On the contrary, the borders that separate one from the other are not based on some reified notion of "Judaism" on the one side and "Christianity" on the other. "Borders," he writes, "are not given but constructed by power to mask hybridity, to occlude and disown it" (2004, 15). Most invested in ontological separation and the closing of borders to movement and the transference of ideas are scholars, be it those heresiologists of the late antique period whom Boyarin has examined, or those in the present, the subject of the present study, who insist upon reifying something as unruly and unwieldy as "Jewishness." Ancient heresiologists and modern scholars share the fantasy of tidiness, the desire to impose order on chaos. One of the easiest ways to do this is to avoid ambiguity, to abhor complexity, and to impose retroactively a set of fixed borders defined largely by subsequent theological speculation that seeks to maintain the difference necessary in later periods for identity formation.

This fluidity of boundaries is also clearly on display at the origin of what would eventually become know as Islam. The seventh-century Arabian Peninsula again affords us a glimpse into the complexity of socioreligious formation. The question that we must avoid asking, although one upon which many traditional analyses work, is one of a well- or fully formed Judaism functioning as the midwife of another monotheism. Abraham Geiger (1810–1874), in his *Was hat Mohammad aus dem Judenthume afugenommen* (What did Muhammad take from the Jews), summarizes this view when he implies that Muhammad or the earliest redactors of the Quran employed technical terms "borrowed" from earlier religions as a way to legitimate the new message. He writes, for example,

> It is not enough for us to give a dry meager summary of the passages which appear to have some connection with Judaism, in order to show that Muhammad really possessed a certain knowledge of it, and used it in the establishment of his new religion, and that, further, a comparison with it makes clear many passages in the Quran. Rather is it our task to show how it was bound up with the spirit, the striving and the aims of Muhammad, with the mind of his time and the constitution of his surroundings, and thus to demonstrate the fact that, even if we were deprived of all proofs which undeniably show Judaism to be a source of the Quran, the conjecture that a borrowing from Judaism had taken place would still be a possibility. (1970 [1835], 3)

Geiger here, invoking a rather traditional conceptual model of cultural exchange and interchange, envisages religions and religious traditions as fixed. It is also a model that is potentially lopsided in that it makes (rabbinic) Judaism into a stable entity, whereas that which it "influences," Islam, is perceived to be in a state of flux. Such modeling enables him to argue problematically that Judaism's essence of ethical monotheism is fixed and that rival monotheisms (whether Christianity or Islam) freely borrow and/or take from it. This description of Judaism's essence, it will be recalled from chapter 2 above, was certainly a product of Geiger's immediate intellectual milieu that sought both to legitimize and apologize for Judaism by making it into the spiritual heir of later monotheisms. This construction of Judaism, largely the product of the nineteenth century, could be subsequently projected onto earlier periods. Rather than ask what the contours of Judaism might have looked like in the western Arabian Peninsula during the seventh century CE, the same period in which the Talmud was being redacted in Babylonian academies thousands of miles away, Geiger's model assumes a stability and a uniformity that could not have existed at the time.

In sixth-century Arabia, for example, there is little historical or textual evidence that terms such as "Jew," "Christian," or "Muslim" (or even "Arab") were mutually exclusive markers of identity. As a result, we should be cautious—as Boyarin warned us of examining the borders separating Judaism from Christianity in the late antique period—of projecting later sectarian notions, such as "Arabness" or "Jewishness," onto the period in question. Adding to this complexity, it is important to realize that the so-called Jewish tribes of Arabia were not necessarily "Jewish" in the way that we use this term today, but Jewish Arab tribes, and the Christian ones were Christian Arab tribes. Moreover, we know very little when it comes to the belief structures and religious contours of these groups. Most likely modern Jews or Christians would recognize very little of the practices and liturgy of such tribal groups if they were transported back in time to the Arabian Peninsula. All of this instructs us that we should avoid assuming that race, religion, and ethnicity—largely modern constructs—functioned in the periods before, during, and even immediately after the formative period of Muhammad's movement. "Arab" and other "religious" identities, in other words, were anything but stable or uniform.

The traditional model, unfortunately one that still seems to be regnant, is that religions possess an essence or a spirit that moves throughout history and that manifests itself in various temporal eras and geographic locales. Space is rarely accorded to the conflict that contributes to the construction of perceived normativities. Or, if they are acknowledged, such normativities are often projected from a later age onto the period in question. In sixth- and seventh-century Arabia, however, we have very little indication what "Judaism" looked like, other than the fact that later Muslim sources used these (religious?) designations. If they did exist, assuming that these later sources do not have an ideological ax to grind (which they all do), we most certainly could not label them using the politically loaded term "normative."

Parts or subsets of this inchoate Judaism, perhaps one that even included "Christians," were most likely absorbed into Muhammad's developing framework. Rather than simply call this framework "Islam," it might be more appropriate to use terms that account for the complexity, such as "a shared Judaizing Muhammadan message." What would eventually become Islam, for example, might well have been a set of beliefs, customs, and practices that represented various local "Jewish" and/or "Christian" traditions in the area. And only at a later date, in the eighth and ninth centuries, as the architects of Islam (e.g., hadith collectors, legal experts, historians) began to crystallize their own tradition, was it neatly excised from a Judaism and a Christianity that were then regarded as normative and as existing side by side with Muhammad's Islam. An all too tidy example that is used to show these discrete traditions interacting with one another is the claim that whereas the Jews prayed facing Jerusalem, for example, Muhammad, early in his stay at Medina, had his followers turn and pray facing Mecca, the birthplace of his message. When he did this—obviously a story with much symbolic meaning for later generations—there most certainly would have been "Jews" who joined him, although they were not "converts" in the way we use the term today because they literally had nothing to "convert" to.

A second assumption is that we have very little evidence that Muhammad set himself the express goal of founding a new religion. Although Islam would be worked out, both theologically and legally, in the centuries after his death, none of these later elements was present at the beginning. As many have shown, Muhammad—especially during the early years in Mecca—preached an inclusive monotheistic message that warned the unbelievers that the Day of Judgment was near. He most decidedly did not preach an exclusive and highly developed teaching that we now recognize as Islam (see, e.g., Powers 2009, 3–10; Donner 2010: 56–89).[5] The journey from his original message to the rise of Islam is a very difficult and convoluted one, and it is still by no means clear how it occurred.[6] However, we must be cautious of using a conceptual model, unfortunately one that is all too common, that assumes that Muhammad simply believed in and preached the Islam of later generations.

A third assumption is that we use our modern term "religion," with all its conceptual and taxonomic baggage, to describe these happenings. We have absolutely no idea, however, what the modern term "religion" would have meant in sixth- and seventh-century Arabia.[7] One thing that we can be certain of is that the term, for which there is no equivalent in Arabic, would not mean what we take it to mean today, where it is primarily used to denote some sort of inner or spiritual feeling that is regarded as immune from a variety of cultural, political, social, and ideological forces. As many theorists have demonstrated, "religion" is a term specific to the West, particularly a modern West that has developed a category of the "secular" that gives "religion" shape and generates its articulation (see, e.g., Asad 2003; Fitzgerald 2007).

These three assumptions begin with the wrong premise—namely, that "religion" meant in sixth-century Arabia what it does today and that, as such, the three sociocultural groups in the Arabian Peninsula formed themselves neatly and tidily into something we can now recognize as discrete religious traditions. Such traditional conceptual modeling is responsible for creating and reifying social groups and their various fluid constructions and dismantlings of identity, making such constructions into natural categories as opposed to social taxonomies. Rather than ask what the contours of religious, ethnic, and social identities were in the period in question, scholarship tends to exacerbate the problem by assuming that all three of these "religious traditions" are somehow stable or essential constructs.

Any discussion of the collisions, overlap, and interactions of these three "religions" or, better, social movements, must recognize—especially in earlier periods—their inner fluidity and the instability of boundaries between them. What, for example, do the varieties of Judaisms and Christianities look like in sixth- and seventh-century Arabia? Are they discrete religious traditions in the way that we think of each of these traditions today? Is Judaism an ethnic or a cultural marker in the sixth-century as it is, say, in a post-1948 world? Is Christological speculation in sixth-century Arabia simply a reflection of what was then emerging as "orthodox" in either the Byzantine or the Roman churches? Even the term "Islam" is implicated in this conceptual difficulty. At what point, for instance, does Islam emerge as the "five-pillared" and theologically worked out tradition of later centuries?

What started out as a "Jewish" tribe, for example, on the eve of Muhammad's preaching, might well have ended up as "Muslim" in the century or so after his death. The crossing of this boundary has nothing to do with conversion, but with a shifting set of ideas and social practices that were in flux and that only became stable at a later date. Rather than simplicity (i.e., "the Jews gave the world ethical monotheism"), we need to account for complexity; and opposed to a retroactively imposed clarity, we need to be aware of the distortion that our categories introduce. Rather than regard Judaism, Christianity, and Islam as three discrete traditions in the early seventh century, it might be more productive to envisage them, using the language of J. Z. Smith (1982, 1–18), polythetically or, using the language of Boyarin, as occupying the same social and cultural space. That is, rather than employing a taxon wherein all subgroups of a given tradition (e.g., Islam) share a common essence while differing from those other closely adjacent taxa (Judaism or Christianity), it might make more sense to conceive of a taxon that consists of a set of properties wherein various subgroups of all three traditions might possess a large number of them, but none of which are seen as essential and possessed by the others.

In the case of Muhammad's Arabia, this leads to the assumption that the three "religions" existed in seventh-century Arabia in the same manner that they do today. This means that terms that we are quite happy employing—such as "religion," "ethnicity," "identity," "multicultural"—are assumed to exist in the same manner that they do today in different times and in different places. I tried to show that this is not the case. Rather, these three modern constructs begin to break down when applied to the Arabian Peninsula on the eve of Islam's rise.

The Construction of Jewish Data

As the previous section has shown, Jewish studies has a lot to offer cognate areas within the humanities. An emphasis on cultural studies, identity formation, and the imposition and maintenance of fixed borders has the potential to open up the way we imagine and classify data that we not unproblematically construct as "Jewish." Unfortunately, however, the apologetics that has governed the construction of such data has been done with the same sort of zeal as employed by Boyarin's "border markers," those late antique heresiologists responsible for determining what fits where on each side of the Judeo-Christian border. The academic decision or consensus concerning what counts as "Jewish" (and, alternatively, what does not) is ultimately an ideological act, one that certainly reflects the larger political contexts in which Jewish communities have lived in the modern world.

The study of Jewish data, its proximity to the emergence of other monotheisms, provides an excellent example of the manifold ways in which identity is created and maintained. It is largely the role of scholars, I suggested above, who reify disciplinary boundaries—topic "x" counts as Jewish studies and must be studied by those who specialize in Jewish data; topic "y," on the other hand, is Christian or Islamic and must be studied by those specializing in these other areas. The result is academic apartheid (see Chidester 1996), as data constructed as meaningful is artificially partitioned between equally artificially constructed disciplines.

The result is that no one working in, say, the rise of Christianity or the rise of Islam ought to be able to study their data as if it were unconnected to the academic study of Judaism, and vice versa. Jewish studies, in other words, ought not to hide itself or be forced to hide by other disciplinary configurations in such a manner that it becomes an enclave of ethnic and religious pride. This is the way it has functioned for much of its history, and as I tried to show in the chapters above, there are real historical, intellectual, and sociological reasons for this. But despite these reasons, the intellectual health and vitality of Jewish studies means that it is time to resituate itself within the academy. The way to go about this, as I suggested above, is to avoid reification whether of data constructed as Jewish or of a self-imposed disciplinary center. Judaism, after all, is not a given in the natural world; it is something that is constructed and contested, imagined and reimagined, by various actors who seek to create something that accords with their ideology using the rhetoric of authenticity, of identity, and of scholarship.

The academic study of Judaism potentially has much to learn from those critical discourses produced within the academic study of religion. By these discourses, I do not refer to the typical phenomenological or ecumenical models that have done so much to shape religious studies, models of which I was largely critical in the introduction, but those that seek to contest the regnant discourses and the interpretive frameworks of the status quo. These regnant discourses have done much to occlude the academic study of Judaism from religious studies, with their implicit supersessionism and emphases on experience over law and other sociocultural forms.

In this chapter, I have largely focused on the role of "Jewish" forms and subcultures in the rise of rival monotheisms. My goal in doing this was to suggest one possible avenue of exploration, one that does not insist on the reification of what is "Jewish" and what is "non-Jewish." This need not be the only way to invoke a renewed Jewish studies within the academic study of religion, however. Even in later centuries, as the taxonomic lines between Jewish and non-Jewish begin to harden somewhat, they never solidify. Once again, then, we must resist the temptation of assuming that communities simply constitute themselves around essential and sui generis qualities. What did the borders among Jews, Muslims, and Christians look like in eleventh-century al-Andalus? Were there sets of features or traits that absolutely defined who was what? It certainly was neither language nor culture—as all partook of Arabic, and all were largely Arabophone. Even when it came to religion, Jews and Christians articulated their religion in Arabic using the categories of that language and all of the baggage that it carried. David Nirenberg, for example, has examined how Jewish historiography, primarily in the aftermath of the Christian persecutions in Spain in 1391, began to fix taxonomic categories such as "Jew" and "Christian." In sorting through the shards of identity between 1391 and 1492, the date at which both Jews and Muslims were expelled from the newly created Spain, he argues that "genealogy [was elevated] to a primary form of communal memory" (2002, 7).

Rather than assume that identities in the premodern world are fixed and inherited in predetermined ways, we ought to be aware of the ways in which they are invented, reinvented, enforced, and patrolled. In this, they are not unlike modern identity formations. Jewish, Christian, and Muslim identities in al-Andalus, as indeed in many other historical periods, were always contingent, constantly in need of maintenance, reinvention, and repair (J. Boyarin 2008). Theories of identity and the shaping of difference are based on theories of self that are produced through various discourses of othering.

The examination of Jewish data must not simply function within the purview of those working in Jewish studies. As a diasporic civilization and as a minority within larger nations and civilization, the study of Jews and of Jewish data, *when properly conceived,* should ideally be of interest to anyone working in humanities-based disciplines.

Conclusions

This chapter, informed by the discussion in the previous five chapters, has attempted to be forward-looking. Rather than focus on apologetical agendas of previous generations and that still function in the field—whether to demonstrate that Jews possess a history or to show how Judaism provides the bedrock of western civilization—this chapter has tried to articulate how Jewish studies can inform and be informed by cognate disciplines. With this in mind, the present chapter sought to show how the very decisions that govern the selection of data—what is "Jewish" and what is not—are not simple reflections of the natural world. Jewish data, in other words, does not exist "out there," waiting to be discovered and described. Such data, on the contrary, is brought into existence by a series of hermeneutical and taxonomic acts. Such acts, in turn, are predicated on a set of academic and nonacademic concerns. The construction of Jewish data, as argued above, is certainly connected to the tumultuous existence of Jews in the modern world. Fights against anti-Semitism, legal ostracism, and the concomitant desire for political emancipation and social inclusion are an intimate part of the story of how Judaism has been imagined and constructed in modern academic circles.

If the study of Judaism is insular, I suggested, this is as much the result of centripetal forces as it is of centrifugal ones. This has been responsible for the tendency to reify something that can be problematically referred to as "Jewishness," something that can be variously defined and located historically. More often than not this concept of "Jewishness" is connected to the rhetoric of authenticity and the various arts of perseverance in the face of adversity. This represents a modern iteration of the age-old trope of chosenness.

While such conceptual modeling may well have done a lot to sustain the study of Judaism for much of the past two hundred years, it seems to me that the time is now right for a rethinking of the field of Jewish studies—what it hopes to accomplish and how it perceives itself in relation to other disciplines and vice versa. My intention in asking these questions was not to suggest that the study of Judaism or Jewish data somehow lags behind the study of other religions or religious forms. On the contrary, it has been to show something of how the study of Judaism came to be: what questions have traditionally motivated it and why? Struggles between insiders and outsiders, critics and caretakers, and the tendency to essentialize a spirit that guides one's data are certainly not unique to the academic study of Judaism.

Rather it is the tension between Jewish data and the critical discourses of the larger discipline of religious studies that has been behind the present study. My colleagues in theory and method in the latter discipline tend to gravitate away from Judaism, preferring to hold the opinion that the academic study of Judaism has little to contribute to the academic study of religion. The previous study has been my answer to them. Certainly, they are correct in the sense that there has been a tendency, perhaps an overwhelming tendency, in Jewish studies toward insularity. However, as I argued, there are real historical and sociological reasons for this. These reasons, however, need not mean that the past is the only way that things must be.

At the same time, many in Jewish studies tend to avoid the types of theoretical questions that some of those in religious studies tend to want to ask of data. This chapter has attempted to bring some of these questions to the forefront. What are some of the reasons that Jewish data has been constructed in the way that it has? And how, looked at afresh, can Judaism, a Judaism with porous and fluid boundaries, illumine data from across the religious studies spectrum? Framed in this manner, Jewish studies and Jewish data have much to offer the academic study of religion.

Jewish studies, in the final analysis, currently stands at a cross-roads. I hope that this study has articulated not only what this cross-roads is, but how we came to stand in front of it. Jewish studies, for much of its history, has existed in the margins. In Germany, Wissenschaft des Judentums formed an academy within an academy, a space in which Jewish scholars of Jewish data could be kept outside of the domain of the university system. In America, especially until the midtwentieth century, Jewish studies sought a foothold within the academy and largely did so owing to the financial benefaction of private donors. Both of these models, however, came with a cost, and both left their indelible mark on the field.

The future, however, is one of infinite possibility. To encounter or embrace this successfully, Jewish studies must confront its past. It is but one aspect of this confrontation that the present study has attempted to articulate.

Notes

Introduction

1. For a disturbing case of an individual who did take this as part of his official job description, see the account of Howard Eilberg-Schwartz in Mahler 1994. I certainly do not wish to imply that this is the fate of all those sympathetic to the political beliefs of Eilberg-Schwartz; however, it is disturbing enough to merit mention. This policing of borders will be the subject matter of chapter 5 below.

2. In her *How Judaism Became a Religion* (2011), Leora Batnitzky is also interested in the issue of how modern Jewish thinkers felt compelled to resolve the tension between Judaism and the modern, Protestant category of religion. Her interests, however, reside more in the story of modern Jewish philosophy—indeed, her monograph is subtitled *An Introduction to Modern Jewish Thought*—than in more recent developments in critical discourses of religious studies.

3. Perhaps slightly more scientifically, a perusal of the list of endowed chairs in Jewish studies on the AJS website (http://www.ajsnet.org/chairs. php) reveals that all holders of such chairs are Jewish.

4. Today, however, even this is problematic. One of the recent trends in Talmudic scholarship, for instance, is to try to contextualize the Babylonian Talmud, which was codified in the sixth century CE, within its immediate Iranian and Zoroastrian milieu (see, for example Bakhos and Shayegan 2010).

5. Although as I have tried to demonstrate in another context (Hughes 2010a), this does not so much show the cross-pollination between Jewish and other cultures as much as it does the collapsing of the artificial distinctions between them.

Chapter One

1. "Talmudic" is an adjective coming from the Talmud, which refers to a central text in rabbinic Judaism. There exist two Talmuds: the Yerushalmi, which was codified in the fifth century, and the Babylonian, which was codified in the sixth century.

2. The exception, of course, was the Hebrew Bible or Old Testament. However, this was not constructed as "Jewish" per se, but as the general spiritual backdrop that produced Jesus (see, for example, Heschel 1998, 17–22).

3. His account of the ordeal and his attempt to recover from the physical and emotional scars may be found in his *Drawing Life: Surviving the Unabomber* (1997).

4. In addition to the work under discussion here, see Gelernter 2005 for another example of Hertog's patronage. As it states at the end of this article: "The present article, in different form, was given as a lecture sponsored by Susan and Roger Hertog in New York in October of last year." In the article in question, Gelernter wrote: "Can you be an agnostic or atheist or Buddhist or Muslim and a believing American too? In each case the answer is yes. But to accomplish that feat is harder than most people realize. The Bible is not merely the fertile soil that brought Americanism forth. It is the energy source that makes it live and thrive; that makes believing Americans willing to prescribe freedom, equality, and democracy even for a place like Afghanistan, once regarded as perhaps the remotest region on the face of the globe. If you undertake to remove Americanism from its native biblical soil, you had better connect it to some other energy source potent enough to keep its principles alive and blooming."

5. Roger Hertog, Gelernter's benefactor, has also been the chairman of the board of the Shalem Center in Jerusalem. Although I shall have more to say about this institution in chapter 5, fellow neoconservative Irving Kristol remarks that it was founded as Israel's first neoconservative think tank, with the aim of giving "the Israeli right a better foundation in history, economics, archaeology and other topics" (Erlanger 2005).

6. This is why, for example, I have such a hard time with local rabbis teaching courses in Jewish studies at universities. While they are qualified to administer a congregation, they are not qualified—unless, of course, they also have a PhD in Jewish or religious studies—to teach the material using a larger disciplinary frame. The result is that such classes often amount to little more than catechesis and a setting in which Jewish students can take "academic" courses with their local rabbi for credit. Such courses, I submit, have no business being taught in a secular university.

7. This, of course, is not unique to Jews and Judaism. Every ethnicity and nationality ultimately constructs itself by defining itself in light of others, which it ultimately finds itself superior to or uniquely different from.

8. The most famous example of this is *The Protocols of the Elders of Zion*, which would be published several decades later.

9. Originally entitled *Das Heilige—Über das Irrationale in der Idee des Göttlichen und sein Verhältnis zum Rationalen* ["The Holy—On the Irrational in the Idea of the Divine and its Relation to the Rational].

10. Indeed, when the war was over Eliade was forbidden from returning to Romania and instead went to Paris where he befriended Georges Dumezil (1898–1986), another scholar of religion and an individual with ties to French fascism. On Dumezil more specifically, see Lincoln 1991, 231–43.

11. This is certainly not to imply that there have not been more theorists more favorably disposed to Judaism (e.g., Jacob Neusner, J. Z. Smith). These, among others, will be the subject of chapter 4 below.

Chapter Two

1. My interest here is largely with the North American context. The European context is much more complex and related to a host of post-World War II developments.

2. Although the Verein eventually reached a maximum of twenty-five members, the weekly members struggled to get its quorum of ten members, and were often cancelled as a result. Eventually the society reduced the quorum necessary for a meeting to five. They published their own journal, *Zeitschrift für die Wissenschaft des Judentums*, with a limited degree of success. The society eventually disbanded in 1824. Its leader, Eduard Gans, converted to Christianity and was subsequently appointed a professor of law in Berlin in the following year. For an excellent history of the movement, see Schorsch 1994, 205–32.

3. There were certainly precursors to this in the premodern world; see for example, Judah Messer Leon (ca. 1425–1498). See also Tirosh-Rothschild 1991, 11–33; Hughes 2007, 108–14.

4. Interestingly, Graetz himself had been accused of being an "Oriental" by the antisemitic historian Heinrich von Treitschke: "Herr Graetz is a foreigner on the soil of his 'accidental land of birth,' an Oriental, who neither understands nor wants to understand the [German] people; he has nothing in common with us other than the fact that he possesses our rights as citizens and uses our native language—although to malign us." In *Der "Berliner Antisemitismusstreit" 1879–1881: Kommentierte Quellenedition*, edited by Karsten Krieger (Berlin: de Gruyter, 2004), vol. 1, 125.

5. This concept of ethical monotheism as the defining essence of Judaism, as I showed in the previous chapter, is still alive and well in many academic circles today.

6. Reform Judaism, for those not familiar with it, is a branch of Judaism that dates, roughly, to the period of Geiger. Articulated through a series of "platforms," it became a movement that held that Jewish belief and practices—and, thus, Judaism—should be modernized and compatible with participation in the larger culture in which Jews found themselves. For Reform Judaism, *halakhah* ("Jewish law") should be interpreted as a set of general guidelines rather than as a list of restrictions whose literal observance is required of all Jews.

7. His basic outline of the study of kabbalah may be found in Scholem 1995 [1941].

8. Scholem was also a regular attendee at the annual gathering of the Eranos conference near Ascona, Switzerland. The goal of this gathering was to bring together scholars of different religious traditions to discuss themes related to religion and spirituality. It was associated with Carl Jung and many

of the themes discussed in the conferences reflected his particular interest in religious symbolism and mythology. Other important figures included Mircea Eliade, Henri Corbin, Karl Lowith, and Paul Tillich (see Wasserstrom 1999). This conference, according to Magid, "proved to be an important outlet for Scholem to move beyond his more parochial studies in Israel and explore the areas of comparative religion and phenomenology that interested him in his youth. It also enabled him to return to a more cosmopolitan European and international setting and present his more specific Hebraic research to a new audience" (Magid 2008).

Chapter Three

1. A highly readable account of this may be found in Elon 2002.

2. For the sake of convenience, I hereafter refer to the mandate period as Israel even though this is anachronistic.

3. Recall in this regard Heilman's comments concerning the need for a director of a Jewish studies program—or, at least, a non-Jewish director of a Jewish studies program—to know this language.

4. Excellent accounts may be found in, among other places, Harris 1991, Schorsch 1994, Myers 1995.

5. This, of course, was not so much a concern among scholars in Israel. There, the issue was not the desire to find inclusion within the larger society, but how to deal with the local Arab populations. And many scholars, most notably, Gershom Scholem, argued for the peaceful coexistence of Arabs and Jews. For the larger context, see Myers 2009.

6. On the history of the AAJR, see their website at http://www.aajr.org/history.

7. Such practices were eventually discontinued when, one year, a female academic—Jane Gerber—stood up and led the prayer. Since the strongest proponents of such religious practices at the AJS would oppose a woman leading such a prayer, the practice was quickly suspended.

8. Both of these papers were written for the proceedings, and were not delivered at the actual colloquium.

9. George Hoffman, a German scholar of Judaica, lamented that there was not a single chair in Jewish studies at German universities. Such chairs, he believed, would dispel anti-Semitic prejudices.

10. In fact, some of the major programs in Jewish studies are today named after such benefactors: the Robert A. and Sandra S. Borns Program (Indiana University), the Samuel and Jean Frankel Center (University of Michigan), the Joseph and Rebecca Meyerhoff Center (University of Maryland), the Taube Center (Stanford), and the Herbert D. Katz Center for Advanced Judaic Studies (University of Pennsylvania), to name but a few.

11. This is certainly not unique to Jewish studies. I remember interviewing for a chair in Islamic studies at the University of Alberta in Edmonton, Canada, which was named the Edmonton Council of Muslim Communities

(ECMC) Chair in Islamic Studies. The very name of this chair is telling of its perceived mandate and the relationship that the holder should, at least ideally, have with the local Muslim community.

12. See, for example, the situation in which Howard Eilberg Schwartz got himself into when he could not, in good conscience, support the Zionistic tendencies of the local Jewish community (see Mahler 1994).

13. See, for example, the list on the Association for Jewish Studies (AJS), the major organization for the academic study of Judaism at http://www.ajsnet.org/chairs.php?id=4.

Chapter Four

1. This includes such support as endowing faculty lines, lectureships, student scholarships, and the like.

2. The Charles and Lynn Schusterman Family Foundation (CLSFF), for example, defines their mandate as "Through our national office in Washington, DC, CLSFF supports programs that ensure vibrant Jewish life by empowering young Jews to embrace the joy of Judaism, build inclusive Jewish communities, support the State of Israel and repair the world" (http://www.schusterman.org/meet-us/mission-values).

3. According to their website, "The mission of the Tikvah Fund is to promote serious Jewish thought about the enduring questions of human life and the pressing challenges that confront the Jewish people. Tikvah will support many programs, projects, and individuals—including new university centers and courses, books and journals, summer seminars and scholarships. Tikvah's work will be grounded in these fundamental convictions: that the great ideas, texts, and traditions of Judaism are a special inheritance, with much to teach everyone in search of wisdom about the human condition; and that the fate of the Jewish people greatly depends on the education of intellectual, religious, and political leaders, both in Israel and the Diaspora" (http://tikvahfund.org/about/).

4. "The Posen Foundation works internationally as a service provider to support secular Jewish education and educational initiatives on Jewish culture in the modern period and the process of Jewish secularization over the past three centuries. At a time when the majority of world Jewry defines itself as secular and is not well educated in Jewish culture, the Foundation offers this growing community the opportunity to deepen and enrich the study of its cultural and historic heritage—from a secular, scholarly perspective" (http://www.posenlibrary.com/frontend/posen-foundation).

5. This certainly is not meant to imply that this is the only disciplinary unit in which the study of Judaism is carried out. There exist positions in departments of history, sociology, English, and film studies, to name but a few. I would, however, argue that religious studies tends to be the natural unit for this. To reiterate, the present study is primarily concerned with the interface between the study of Judaism and that of religious studies.

6. I should make it clear that I do not consider the models employed and deployed within the larger field of religious studies to be unproblematic or themselves based on a host of unchecked assumptions. See, for example, the studies of McCutcheon 1999; Fitzgerald 2000; Smith 1990; Smith 1998.

7. The American Academy of Religion (AAR), today the largest organization devoted to the study of religion in both North America and the world, was only founded in 1963. Previously it had been known as the National Association of Biblical Instructors (NABI). Not coincidentally, the name change from NABI to AAR occurred in the immediate aftermath of the *Abington School District vs. Schempp* Supreme Court case that attempted to differentiate between "teaching religion" and "teaching *about* religion." See J. Z. Smith 2004, 197–202, and Lincoln 2012, 131–36.

8. Online at http://www.aarweb.org/programs/ALHR/default.asp.

9. This seems to be true even until the 1960s. All of the essays in the proceedings from the first AJS colloquium in 1969 (Jick 1970) deal with premodern Judaism with the exception of that by Marshall Sklare.

10. Recall here William James' famous line: "It is true that we instinctively recoil from seeing an object to which our emotions and our affections are committed handled by the intellect as any other object is handled. The first thing the intellect does with an object is to class it along with something else. But any object that is infinitely important to us and awakens our devotion feels to us also as if it must be sui generis and unique. Probably a crab would be filled with a sense of personal outrage if it could hear us class it without ado or apology as a crustacean, and thus dispose of it. 'I am no such thing,' it would say; 'I am MYSELF, MYSELF alone'" (James 1990 [1902], 17).

11. This seminary was one of the first institutions that introduced regular historical study into the rabbinic curriculum (Myers 2003, 27). This, of course, meant that the rabbis that this seminary produced were interested not just in the religious texts of Jews, but also in the various historical contexts that produced them.

12. Neither was particularly fond of Jews or Judaism. Franz, for example, translated the New Testament into Hebrew and established the Institutum Judaicum for the training of missionary workers among Jews; whereas Friedrich argued that the Bible had copied numerous Babylonian and Assyrian myths and that Germanic myths should replace Old Testament ones in schools. Indeed, one of Friedrich's students, Paul Haupt, later to be the director of the Oriental Seminary at Johns Hopkins, could argue that Jesus was an Aryan and not a Semite (see Heschel 2008, 57)

13. Much like Jastrow, Tiele was a scholar of Assyrian, Egyptian, and Semitic religions. His *Outlines of the History of Religion* (1877) had had a huge impact on English-speaking audiences, as did his Gifford Lectures from 1896–1897, entitled "Elements in the Science of Religion."

14. See http://query.nytimes.com/mem/archive-free/pdf?_r=1&res=98 04E4DE1238E633A2575BC1A9649C946496D6CF&oref=slogin.

15. From the series description at http://press.princeton.edu/catalogs/series/bs.html.

16. A Wikipedia entry calls him "one of the most published authors in history." See http://en.wikipedia.org/wiki/Jacob_Neusner.

17. Not to mention the fact that many scholars in the field are also highly critical of Neusner's own interpretation of rabbinic texts. See, for example, Lieberman 1984; Sanders 1990.

18. Boyarin takes an even more extreme point in his recent *The Jewish Gospels* (2012), wherein he argues that "Judaism" as a "religion" only becomes possible with the advent of "Christianity."

Chapter Five

1. In addition to the collection of essays in Gotzmann and Wiese 2007, see Myers 1993.

2. Because my concern in this study is how Judaism is situated within the academic study of religion, I have rarely touched upon the academic study of Israel or, as it is more customarily known, Israel studies. As one could imagine the study of Israel, from various disciplinary perspectives (e.g., history, political science, anthropology, geography), has the potential for tremendous controversy. I will touch occasionally upon some of these controversies in this chapter, but I think it important to be clear and articulate at the outset that Israel studies is *not* simply an Israel advocacy discipline, although in the hands of some it can certainly become this.

3. Indeed, both the Tikvah fund and the Posen Foundation (under the name Center for Cultural Judaism) are "institutional members" of the Association for Jewish Studies (AJS), two outliers among what are otherwise university departments or centers. See http://www.ajsnet.org/institutions_members.htm.

4. See, for example, http://www.brandeis.edu/israelcenter/about/index.html.

5. http://hebrewjudaic.as.nyu.edu/object/taubpostdocs.

6. "Post-Zionism," perhaps not surprisingly, has numerous meanings. Some use it pejoratively in the sense of anti-Zionism, in which case to label an individual as an "anti-Zionist" is to argue that they are against the State of Israel. A more nuanced sense of the term can be that Zionism fulfilled its mission with the formation of the State of Israel and that it is now time to move beyond it. This, obviously, has repercussions on the religious makeup of the country, the treatment of Palestinians, and so on.

7. See, for example, http://www.schusterman.org/programs/community/jewish-studies-expansion-project.

8. http://www.h-net.org/announce/show.cgi?ID=155676.

9. http://jewishculture.org/jsep.

10. http://zeek.forward.com.

11. http://zeek.forward.com/about.

12. In 2009, for example, the slogan of Lieberman's party, Yisrael Beiteinu, was "No loyalty, no citizenship," meaning that all Israelis, including

Arab citizens, ought to swear loyalty to the Jewish state if they wanted to be citizens.

13. The AJC, one of the oldest Jewish advocacy organizations in the United Sates, according to its website, was established in 1906. It argues that "the best way to protect Jewish populations in danger would be to work towards a world in which all peoples were accorded respect and dignity . . . AJC continues its efforts to promote pluralistic and democratic societies where all minorities are protected. AJC is an international think tank and advocacy organization that attempts to identify trends and problems early—and take action. Our key areas of focus are:

- Combating anti-Semitism and all forms of bigotry;

- Promoting pluralism and shared democratic values;

- Supporting Israel's quest for peace and security;

- Advocating for energy independence;

- Strengthening Jewish life" (http://www.ajc.org/site/c.ijITI2 PHKoG/b.789093/k.124/Who_We_Are.htm).

14. For a critique of Rosenfeld's position, see the comments of Shaul Magid, "Why Must Jews Support a Jewish State?" *Zeek* Online at at http:// zeek.net/704debate.

15. Even when the Palestinian-Israeli conflict is not mentioned it can still seem odd. In his recent and elegant theology of Judaism (2008), Michael Fishbane makes absolutely no mention of how this conflict impinges upon not only the State of Israel, but also worldwide Jewry. It strikes me that any theological elaboration of Judaism in the twenty-first century has to take the State of Israel's role in this conflict into consideration, whether to critique it or support it.

16. http://www.tikvahfund.org/about/page/our-founder-zalman-c-bernstein.

17. Online at http://www.tikvahfund.org/about.

18. Kramer, for example, is the author of, among other things, a highly critical assessment of Islamic studies (2001). In addition, he is a fellow at the AIPAC-established Washington Institute for Near East Policy, which published his aforementioned book.

19. http://www.adelsonfoundation.org/AFF/prf/AdelsonInstitute forStrategicStudies.pdf.

20. http://www.shalem.org.il/Statements/President-s-Message.html.

21. http://sicsa.huji.ac.il.

22. http://sicsa.huji.ac.il.

23. http://www.posenlibrary.com/frontend/posen-foundation.

24. Yale University Press seems to be pretty equal opportunity. Not only does it take subventions from the Posen Foundation for its library, but

it also takes money from Tikvah to support the publication of books it deems worthy (e.g., Gelernter 2009).

25. http://www.posenfoundation.com/academicprograms/grantshighereducation.html.

26. http://posenfoundation.com/what-we-do/posen-project.php.

Chapter Six

1. Concerning the John Templeton Foundation (JTF), Massimo Pigliucci, a professor of philosophy at the City University of New York, writes of the introductory videos that one sees on the Templeton website. "The second concerns 'character development,' which early on features David Myers (Hope College) talking about Templeton's desire that science could eventually study and validate the 'laws of life' (uh?) underlying good living, which led JTF to fund research on 'forgiveness' (clearly a heavily Christian-influenced concept seldom found in the scientific vocabulary, until Templeton started giving out grants to study it). Following that, we have an appearance by David Blankenhorn, of the Institute for American Values, a neoconservative think tank, naturally advocating rather vague 'changes in public policies' stemming from JTF's funded research" (http://rationallyspeaking.blogspot.com/2011_11_01_archive.html).

2. In this respect I note that the major conversation that Tikvah wants to have with other disciplines is in the great books curriculum read through a particular right-wing agenda.

3. Geertz, years ago, warned us of moving away from small, real-time events in favor of more grandiose efforts of "discovering the Continent of Meaning and mapping out its bodiless landscape" (1973, 20).

4. The rest of this section reworks Hughes 2013, 118–40.

5. Although both Donner and Powers agree that the formation of Islam is complicated, it is worth noting that their basic premises are radically different.

6. In Islamic studies circles, this is known as the "Authenticity Debate." There exist at least three different perspectives in this debate. The first contends that even though the earliest sources of Islam may come from a later period, they nonetheless represent reasonably reliable accounts concerning the matters upon which they comment or describe.

Another perspective contends that the Muslim historical record of the first two centuries is historically problematic. The social and political upheavals associated with the rapid spread of Islam fatally compromise, according to such scholars, the earliest sources. These sources, according to this position, are written so much after the fact and with such distinct ideological or political agendas that they provide us with very little that is reliable and with which to recreate the period upon which they purport to describe.

The third perspective acknowledges the problems involved with the early sources but tries to solve them using form and source criticism, both of which seek to determine the original form and historical context of a particular text.

A survey and analysis of these competing positions may be found in Berg 2000, 6–64.

7. This is my problem with Donner's book, which uses terms such as "belief," "religion," and even "spirituality" to refer to Muhammad's Arabia.

Works Cited

Alles, Gregory D. 1996. "Introduction." In Gregory D. Alles, ed. and trans., *Rudolf Otto: Autobiographical and Social Essays*, 1–48. The Hague: Walter de Gyuyter.

Altmann, Alexander. 1980. "Jewish Studies: Their Scope and Meaning." In Raphael Jospe and Samuel Z. Fishman, eds., *Go and Study: Essays in Honor of Alfred Jospe*, 83–98. Washington: B'nai B'rith Hillel Foundations.

Asad, Talal. 2003. *Formations of the Secular: Christianity, Islam, Modernity*. Stanford: Stanford University Press.

Bäck, Samuel. 1906. *Die Geschichte des jüdischen Volkes und seiner Literatur vom babylonischen Exil bis auf die Gegenwart*, 3rd ed. Frankfurt am Main: J. Kauffmann.

Bakhos, Carol, and Rahim Shayegan, eds. 2010. *The Talmud in Its Iranian Context*. Tübingen: Mohr Siebeck.

Band, Arnold J. 1966. "Jewish Studies in American Liberal-Arts Colleges and Universities." *American Jewish Yearbook* 67: 1–30.

Baron, Salo Wittmeyer. 1952–1983. *A Social and Religious History of the Jews*. 18 vols. 2nd ed. New York: Columbia University Press.

Barton, George A. 1921. "The Contributions of Morris Jastrow, Jr. to the History of Religion." *Journal of the American Oriental Society* 41: 327–333.

Batnitzky, Leora. 2011. *How Judaism Became a Religion: An Introduction to Modern Jewish Thought*. Princeton: Princeton University Press.

Bayart, Jean-François. 2005. *The Illusion of Cultural Identity*. Trans. Steven Rendall et al. Chicago: University of Chicago Press.

Berg, Herbert. 2000. *The Development of Exegesis in Early Islam: The Authenticity of Muslim Literature from the Formative Period*. London: Curzon, 2000.

Berger, Adriana. 1994. "Mircea Eliade: Romanian Fascism and the History of Religions in the United States." In Nancy A. Harrowitz, ed., *Tainted Greatness: Antisemitism and Cultural Heroes*, 51–74. Philadelphia: Temple University Press.

Biale, David. 1982. *Gershom Scholem: Kabbalah and Counter-History*, 2nd ed. Cambridge, MA: Harvard University Press, 1982.

———. 2011. *Not in the Heavens: The Tradition of Secular Jewish Thought*. Princeton, NJ: Princeton University Press.

Bland, Kalman P. 2001. *The Artless Jew: Medieval and Modern Affirmations and Denials of the Visual*. Princeton, NJ: Princeton University Press.

Blau, Joseph L. 1970. "A Proposal for a Professional Association." In Leon Jick, ed., *The Teaching of Judaica in American Universities: The Proceedings of a Colloquium*, 89–94. New York: Ktav.

Blumenthal, David J. 1976. "Where Does 'Jewish Studies' Belong?" *Journal of the American Academy of Religion* 44.3: 535–546.

Bodian, Miriam. 1999. *Hebrews of the Portuguese Nation: Conversos and Community in Early Modern Amsterdam*. Bloomington, IN: Indiana University Press.

Bourdieu, Pierre. 1984. *Distinction: A Social Critique of the Judgment of Taste*. Trans. Richard Nice. Cambridge, MA: Harvard University Press.

Boustan, Ra'anan S., Oren Kosansky and Marina Rustow, eds. 2011. *Jewish Studies at the Crossroads of History and Anthropology: Authority, Diaspora, Tradition*. Philadelphia: University of Pennsylvania Press.

Boyarin, Daniel. 2004. *Border Lines: The Partition of Judaeo-Christianity*. Philadelphia: University of Pennsylvania Press.

———. 2012. *The Jewish Gospels: The Story of the Jewish Christ*. New York: The New Press.

Boyarin, Jonathan. 2008. "Responsive Thinking: Cultural Studies and Jewish Historiography." In Boyarin, *Jewishness and the Human Dimension*, 25–44. New York: Fordham University Press.

———. 2009. *The Unconverted Self: Jews, Indians, and the Identity of Christian Europe*. Chicago: University of Chicago Press.

Braiterman, Zachary. 2011. "Conservative Money and Jewish Studies: Investigating the Tikvah Fund." *Zeek: A Jewish Journal of Thought and Culture*. Online at http://www.zeek.forward.com/articles/117374.

Branscomb, Harvey. 1970. "A Note on Establishing Chairs of Jewish Studies." In Leon Jick, ed., *The Teaching of Judaica in American Universities: The Proceedings of a Colloquium*, 94–99. New York: Ktav.

Brenner, Michael. 2010. *Prophets of the Past: Interpreters of Jewish History*. Translated by Steven Rendall. Princeton, NJ: Princeton University Press.

Budde, Karl. 1899. *Religion of Israel to the Exile*. London and New York: G. P. Putnam's Sons.

Bush, Andrew. 2011. *Jewish Studies: A Theoretical Introduction*. New Brunswick, NJ: Rutgers University Press.

Cahill, Thomas. 1998. *The Gifts of the Jews: How a Tribe of Desert Nomads Changed the Way Everyone Thinks and Feels*. New York: Anchor Books.

Cheyne, T. K. 1898. *Jewish Religious Life after the Exile*. London and New York: G. P. Putnam's Sons.

Chidester, David. 1996. *Savage Systems: Colonialism and Comparative Religions in Southern Africa*. Charlottesville, VA: University of Virginia Press.

Clay, Albert T., and James A. Montgomery. 1921. "Obituary Notice: Morris Jastrow, Jr." *Proceedings of the American Philosophical Society*. 60.4: x–xxvi.

Cohen, Gerson D. 1997. "Modern Jewish Scholarship and the Continuity of Faith." In Gerson D. Cohen, ed., *Jewish History and Jewish Destiny*. New York: Jewish Theological Seminary of America Press.

Cohen, Hermann. 1975. *Religion of Reason Out of the Sources of Judaism.* 2nd ed. Translated with an introduction by Simon Kaplan. Atlanta: Scholars Press.

Cohen, Jeremy. 2008. "Introduction." In Jeremy Cohen and Richard I. Cohen, eds., *The Jewish Contribution to Civilization: Reassessing an Idea*, 1–8. Oxford: Littman Library.

Cohen, Jonathan. 2007. *Philosophers and Scholars: Wolfson, Guttmann and Strauss on the History of Jewish Philosophy.* Translated by Rachel Yarden. Lanham, MD: Lexington Books.

Cohen, Richard A. 2010. "Singularity: The Universality of Jewish Particularism—Benamozegh and Levinas." In Richard A. Cohen, *Levinasian Meditations: Ethics, Philosophy, and Religion*, 255–272. Pittsburgh, PA: Duquesne University Press.

Craig, John. E. 1984. *Scholarship and Nation Building: The Universities of Strasbourg and Alsatian Society (1870–1939).* Chicago: University of Chicago Press.

Dan, Joseph. 1994. "Gershom Scholem and Jewish Messianism." In Paul Mendes-Flohr, ed., *Gershom Scholem: The Man and His Work*, 73–86. Albany and Jerusalem: State University of New York Press and the Israel Academy of Sciences and Humanities.

Donner, Fred. 2010. *Muhammad and the Believers: At the Origins of Islam.* Cambridge, MA: Harvard University Press.

Dubuisson, Daniel. 2003. *The Western Construction of Religion: Myths, Knowledge, and Ideology.* Trans. William Sayers. Baltimore, MD: Johns Hopkins University Press.

———. 2006. *Twentieth Century Mythologies.* London Equinox.

Durkheim, Emile. 1968 [1915]. *The Elementary Forms of the Religious Life.* Trans. Joseph Ward Swain. New York: The Free Press.

Eilberg-Schwartz, Howard. 1990. *The Savage in Judaism: An Anthropology of Israelite Religion and Ancient Judaism.* Bloomington, IN: Indiana University Press.

Eliade, Mircea. 1958. *Patterns in Comparative Religion.* Trans. Rosemary Sheed. New York: Meridian.

———. 1959. *The Sacred and the Profane: The Nature of Religion.* Trans. Willard R. Trask. New York: Harvest/HBJ.

Ellinwood Frank F. 1892. *Oriental Religions and Christianity: A Course of Lectures Delivered in the Ely Foundation before the Students of Union Theological Seminary, 1891.* New York: Charles Scribner's Sons.

Elon, Amos. 2002. *The Pity of It All: A Portrait of the German-Jewish Epoch, 1743–1933.* New York: Picador.

Erlanger, Steven. 2005. "The City of David Is Found." *New York Times.* Online at http://www.nytimes.com/2005/08/05/international/middleeast/05jerusalem.html.

Fishbane, Michael. 2008. *Sacred Attunement: A Jewish Theology.* Chicago: University of Chicago Press.

Fitzgerald, Timothy. 2000. *The Ideology of Religious Studies*. New York: Oxford University Press.

———. 2007. *Discourse on Civility and Barbarity: A Critical History of Religion and Related Categories*. New York and Oxford: Oxford University Press.

Frazer, James George. 1950. *The Golden Bough: A Study in Magic and Religion*. Abridged Edition. New York: Macmillan.

Geertz, Clifford. 1973. *The Interpretation of Cultures: Selected Essays*. New York: Basic Books.

Geiger, Abraham. 1970 [1835]. *Judaism and Islam*. Trans. F. M. Young. New York: Ktav.

———. 1985. *Judaism and Its History in Two Parts*. Lanham, MD: University Press of America.

———. 2005 [1835]. *Was hat Mohammed aus dem Judenthume aufgenommen?* Berlin: Parega.

Gelernter, David. 1997. *Drawing Life: Surviving the Unabomber*. New York: The Free Press.

———. 2005. "Americanism—and Its Enemies." *Commentary*. Online at http://www.commentarymagazine.com/article/americanism-and-its-enemies/.

———. 2009. *Judaism: A Way of Being*. New Haven, CT: Yale University Press.

Goodenough, Erwin Ramsdell. 1953–1968. *Jewish Symbols in the Greco-Roman Period*. 13 vols. Princeton, NJ: Princeton University Press.

Gotzmann, Andreas, and Christian Wiese, eds. 2007. *Modern Judaism and Historical Consciousness: Identities, Encounters, Perspectives*. Leiden: Brill.

Graetz, Heinrich. 1956 [1891]. *History of the Jews*. Vol. 3. Philadelphia: Jewish Publication Society of America.

———. 1975. *The Structure of Jewish History and Other Essays*. Translated, edited, and introduced by Ismar Schorsch. New York: Jewish Theological Seminary.

Greenberg, Eric J. 1996. "Debate Rages over Non-Jewish Head of Jewish Studies," *New York Jewish Week*, August 16. Online at http://www.jweekly.com/article/full/3845/debate-rages-over-non-jewish-head-of-jewish-studies.

Greenberg, Irving. 1970. "Scholarship and Continuity: Dilemma and Dialectic." In *The Teaching of Judaica in American Universities: The Proceedings of a Colloquium*, 115–131. New York: Ktav.

Greenspahn, Frederick E. 2000. "The Beginnings of Jewish Studies in American Universities." *Modern Judaism* 20: 209–225.

Harris, Jay. 1991. *Nachman Krochmal: Guiding the Perplexed of the Modern Age*. New York: New York University Press.

Heilman, Samuel C. 1996. "Who Should Direct Jewish Studies at the University?" July 21. Online at http://h-net.msu.edu/cgibin/logbrowse.pl?trx=vx&list=H-Judaic&month=9607&week=d&msg=owar/YAZ0rC9RYi2P3re1g&user=&pw.

Heschel, Susannah. 1998. *Abraham Geiger and the Jewish Jesus*. Chicago: University of Chicago Press.

———. 1998. "Jewish Studies as Counterhistory." In David Biale, Michael Galchinsky, and Susannah Heschel, eds., *Insider/Outsider: American Jews and Multiculturalism*, 101–115. Berkeley: University of California Press.

———. 2008. *The Aryan Jesus: Christian Theologians and the Bible in Nazi Germany*. Princeton, NJ: Princeton University Press.

Horowitz, Sara. 1998. "The Paradox of Jewish Studies in the New Academy." In David Biale, Michael Galchinsky, and Susannah Heschel, eds., *Insider/Outsider: American Jews and Multiculturalism*, 101–115. Berkeley: University of California Press.

Hughes, Aaron W. 2007. *Situating Islam: The Past and Future of an Academic Discipline*. London: Equinox.

———. 2008. *The Art of Dialogue in Jewish Philosophy*. Bloomington, IN: Indiana University Press.

———. 2010a. *The Invention of Jewish Identity: Bible, Philosophy and the Art of Translation*. Bloomington, IN: Indiana University Press.

———. 2010b. "Judaism, Judaisms, Jewish: Toward Redefining Traditional *Taxa*." In Aaron W. Hughes, ed., *Defining Judaism: A Reader*, 1–14. London: Equinox.

———. 2012. *Theorizing Islam: On Disciplinary Deconstruction and Reconstruction*. London: Equinox.

———. 2013. *Abrahamic Religions: On the Uses and Abuses of History*. New York and Oxford: Oxford University Press.

———. forthcoming. *Rethinking Jewish Philosophy: Beyond Particularism and Universalism*. New York and Oxford: Oxford University Press.

Idel, Moshe. 1999. "Academic Studies of Kabbalah in Israel, 1923–1998: A Short Survey." *Studia Judaica* 8.1: 91–114.

Iggers, Georg. 1983. *The German Conception of History: The National Tradition of Historical Thought from Herder to the Present*, revised paperback edition. Middleton, CT: Wesleyan University Press.

IJTH (Institute of Jewish Thought and Heritage). Homepage. Online at http://jewishstudies.buffalo.edu/index.shtml.

James, William. 1990 [1902]. *The Varieties of Religious Experience*. New York: Vintage.

Jastrow, Marcus. 2005 [1903]. *A Dictionary of the Targumim, the Talmud Babli and Yerushalmi, and the Midrashic Literature*. Peabody, MA: Hendrickson.

Jastrow, Jr., Morris. 1885. "Abu Zakarijja Jahja b. Dawud Hajjug und Seine Zwei Grammatischen Schriften über die Verben mit Schwachen Buchstaben und die Verben mit Doppelbuchstaben." *Zeitschrift für die Alttestamentliche Wissenschaft* 5: 192–221.

———. 1899. "The Historical Study of Religions in Universities and Colleges." *Journal of the American Oriental Society* 20, second part (July–December): 317–325.

———. 1902. *The Study of Religion*. New York: Charles Scribner's Sons.

———. 1911. *Aspects of Religious Belief and Practice in Babylonia and Assyria*. New York: Charles Scribner's Sons.

Jick, Leon, ed. 1970. *The Teaching of Judaica in American Universities: The Proceedings of a Colloquium.* New York: Ktav.

Kramer, Martin. 2001. *Ivory Towers on Sand: The Failure of Middle Eastern Studies in America.* Washington: Washington Institute for Near East Policy.

Lambden, Stephen N. n.d. "Thomas Kelly Cheyne (1841–1915), Biblical Scholar and Baha'i." Online at http://www.hurqalya.pwp.blueyonder.co.uk/baha'i%20encyclopedia/thomas_kelly_cheyne.htm.

Lanski, Na'ama, and Daphna Berman. 2007. "Storm in a Neo-con Teapot." *Haaretz* Nov. 29. Online at http://www.haaretz.com/weekend/week-s-end/storm-in-a-neo-con-teapot-1.234226.

Levine, Lee I. 1998. *Judaism and Hellenism in Antiquity: Conflict or Confluence?* Seattle: University of Washington Press.

Levinson, Julian. 2003. "Is There a Jewish Text in This Class? Jewish Modernism in the Multicultural Academy." *Michigan Quarterly Review* 42.1: 1–8. Online at http://hdl.handle.net/2027/spo.act2080.0042.122.

Levy, Richard N. 1974. "The American University and *Olam Ha-Ba.*" *Religious Education* 69: 11–27.

Liberles, Robert. 1995. *Salo Wittmayer Baron: Architect of Jewish History.* New York: New York University Press.

Lieberman, Saul. 1984. "A Tragedy or a Comedy?" *Journal of the American Oriental Society,* 104.2: 315–319.

Lincoln, Bruce. 1991. *Death, War, and Sacrifice: Studies in Ideology and Practice.* Chicago: University of Chicago Press.

———. 1994. *Authority: Construction and Corrosion.* Chicago: University of Chicago Press.

———. 1996. "Theses on Method." *Method and Theory in the Study of Religion* 8.3: 225–227.

———. 1999. *Theorizing Myth: Narrative, Ideology, and Scholarship.* Chicago: University of Chicago Press.

———. 2012. *Gods and Demons, Priests and Scholars: Critical Explorations in the History of Religions.* Chicago: University of Chicago Press.

Loveland, Kristen. 2008. "The Association for Jewish Studies: A Brief History." Online at http://www.ajsnet.org/ajs.pdf.

Mack, Michael. 2003. *German Idealism and the Jew: The Inner Anti-Semitism of Philosophy and German-Jewish Responses.* Chicago: University of Chicago Press.

Magid, Shaul. 2008. "Gershom Scholem." *Stanford Encyclopedia of Philosophy.* Online at http://plato.stanford.edu/entries/scholem.

Mahler, Jonathan. 1994. "Howard's End: Why a Leading Jewish Studies Scholar Gave Up His Career." *Lingua Franca.* March. 51–57

Marx, Karl. 1844. "The Jewish Question." In Robert C. Tucker, ed., *The Marx-Engels Reader,* 24–51. New York: Norton.

Marchand, Suzanne L. 2009. *German Orientalism in the Age of Empire: Religion, Race, and Scholarship.* Cambridge: Cambridge University Press.

Masuzawa, Tomoko. 2005. *The Invention of World Religions: Or, How Universalism Was Preserved in the Language of Pluralism.* Chicago: University of Chicago Press.

McCutcheon, Russell T. 1997. *Manufacturing Religion: The Discourse on Sui Generis Religion and the Politics of Nostalgia.* New York: Oxford University Press.

———. 2001. *Critics not Caretakers: Redescribing the Public Study of Religion.* Albany: State University of New York Press.

———. 2003. "The Ideology of Closure and the Problem with the Insider/Outsider Problem In the Study of Religion." *Studies in Religion/ Sciences religieuses* 32.3: 337–352.

———. 2005. *Religion and the Domestication of Dissent: Or, How to Live in a Less than Perfect Nation.* London: Equinox.

———. 2012. "A Tale of Nouns and Verbs: A Rejoinder to Ann Taves." *Journal of the American Academy of Religion.*

Moore, George Foot. 1919. *History of Religions. Volume Two: Judaism, Christianity, Mohammedanism.* New York: Charles Scribner's Sons.

———. 1955 [1927]. *Judaism in The First Centuries of the Christian Era: The Age of the Tannaim.* Volume One. Cambridge, MA: Harvard University Press.

Myers, David N. 1995. *Re-Inventing the Jewish Past: European Jewish Intellectuals and the Zionist Return to History.* New York and Oxford: Oxford University Press.

———. 2003. *Resisting History: Historicism and Its Discontents in German-Jewish Thought.* Princeton, NJ: Princeton University Press.

———. 2009. *Between Jew and Arab: The Lost Voice of Simon Rawidowicz.* Lebanon, NH: University Press of New England for Brandeis University Press.

Neusner, Jacob. 1970. *A Life of Yohanan ben Zakkai, ca. 1–80CE.* 2nd ed. compl. rev. Leiden: Brill.

———. 1979. "Map without Territory: Mishnah's System of Sacrifice and Sanctuary." *History of Religions* 19: 103–127.

———. 1988. *Judaism: The Evidence of the Mishnah.* 2nd edition. Atlanta: Scholars Press.

———. 1995. *The Documentary Foundation of Rabbinic Culture: Mopping Up after Debates with Gerald L. Bruns, S. J. D. Cohen, Arnold Maria Goldberg, Susan Handelman, Christine Hayes, James Kugel, Peter Schäfer, Eliezer Segal, E. P. Sanders, and Lawrence H. Schiffman.* Atlanta: Scholars Press for South Florida Studies in the History of Judaism.

Nirenberg, "David. 2002. "Mass Conversion and Genealogical Mentalities: Jews and Christian in Fifteenth-Century Spain." *Past and Present* 174: 3–41.

Nochlin, Linda, and Tamar Garb, eds. 1996. *The Jew in the Text: Modernity and the Construction of Identity.* London: Thames and Hudson.

Norwood, Stephen H. 2009. *The Third Reich in the Ivory Tower: Complicity and Conflict on American Campuses.* Cambridge: Cambridge University Press.

Orsi, Robert A. 1999. Introduction: Crossing the City Line." In Robert A. Orsi, ed., *Gods of the City: Religion and the American Urban Landscape,* 1–78. Bloomington, IN: Indiana University Press.

———. 2005. *Between Heaven and Earth: The Religious Worlds People Make and the Scholars Who Study Them.* Princeton, NJ: Princeton University Press.

Otto, Rudolph. 1908. *The Life and Ministry of Jesus, according to the critical method: Being a Course of Lectures*. Trans. H. J. Whitby. Chicago: Open Court.

———. 1958 [1917]. *The Idea of the Holy*. Trans. John W. Harvey. New York and Oxford: Oxford University Press.

Pals, Daniel. 1996. *Seven Theories of Religion*. New York: Oxford University Press.

Powers, David. 2009. *Muhammad Is Not the Father of Any of Your Men: The Making of the Last Prophet*. Philadelphia: University of Pennsylvania Press.

Prothero, Stephen. 2010. *God Is Not One: The Eight Rival Religions That Run the World—and Why Their Differences Matter*. New York: HarperCollins.

Proudfoot, Wayne. 1985. *Religious Experience*. Berkeley: University of California Press.

Ringer, Fritz K. 1969. *The Decline of the German Mandarins: The German Academic Community, 1890–1933*. Cambridge, MA: Harvard University Press.

Ritterbrand, Paul, and Harold S. Wechsler. 1994. *Jewish Learning in American Universities: The First Century*. Bloomington, IN: Indiana University Press.

Rosenfeld, Alvin. 2006. *"Progressive" Jewish Thought and the New Anti-Semitism*. American Jewish Committee. Online at http://www.ajc.org/fat/cf/%7B42D75369-D582-4380-8395-D25925B85EAF%7D/PROGRESSIVE_JEWISH_THOUGHT.PDF.

Rosenzweig, Franz. 2005. *The Star of Redemption*. Translated by Barbara E. Galli. Madison, WI: University of Wisconsin Press.

Sanders, E. P. 1990. *Jewish Law from Jesus to the Mishnah: Five Studies*. Philadelphia: Trinity Press.

Sandmel, Samuel. 1970. "Scholar or Apologist?" In Leon Jick, ed., *The Teaching of Judaica in American Universities: The Proceedings of a Colloquium*, 101–111. New York: Ktav.

Scharf, Robert. 1999. "Experience." In Mark C. Taylor, ed., *Critical Terms for Religious Studies*, 70–93. Chicago: University of Chicago Press.

Scholem, Gershom. 1971a. "The Science of Judaism—Then and Now." In *The Messianic Idea in Judaism and Other Essays on Jewish Spirituality*, 304–313. New York: Schocken.

———. 1971b. "Toward an Understanding of the Messianic Idea in Judaism." In *The Messianic Idea and Other Essays on Jewish Spirituality*, 1–36. New York: Schocken.

———. 1995 [1941]. *Major Trends in Jewish Mysticism*. 2nd ed. with a new forward by Robert Alter. New York: Schocken.

———. 1997. "Reflections on Modern Jewish Studies." In Avraham Shapira, ed., Jonathan Chipman, trans., *On the Possibility of Jewish Mysticism in Our Time and Other Essays*, 51–71. Philadelphia: Jewish Publication Society of America.

Schorsch, Ismar, 1994. *From Text to Context: The Turn to History in Modern Judaism*. Waltham, MA: Brandeis University Press.

Schwartz, Seth. 2002. "Historiography on the Jews in the 'Talmudic Period' (70–640 CE)." In Martin Goodman, ed., *The Oxford Handbook of Jewish Studies*, 79–114. Oxford: Oxford University Press.

Schwarz, Leo. 1965. "A Bibliographic Essay." In Saul Lieberman, ed., *Harry Austryn Jubilee Volume* I, 1–46. Jerusalem: American Academy for Jewish Research.

Segal, Eliezer. 2009. *Introducing Judaism*. London and New York: Routledge.

Simon, Marcel. 1975. "The Religionsgeschichte Schule Fifty Years Later." *Religious Studies* 11.2: 135–144.

Smith, Jonathan Z. 1978. *Map Is Not Territory: Studies in the History of Religions*. Chicago: University of Chicago Press.

———. 1982. *Imagining Religion: From Babylon to Jonestown*. Chicago: University of Chicago Press.

———. 1990. *Drudgery Divine: On the Comparison of Early Christianities and the Religions of Late Antiquity*. Chicago: University of Chicago Press.

———. 1998. "Religion, Religions, Religious." In Mark C. Taylor, *Critical Terms for Religious Studies*, 269–284. Chicago: University of Chicago Press.

———. 2004. *Relating Religion: Essays in the Study of Religion*. Chicago: University of Chicago Press.

Steinschneider, Moritz. "Die Zukunft der jüdischen Wissenschaft," *Hebräische Bibliographie* 9 (1869): 76–78.

Steinweis, Alan E. 2008. *Studying the Jew: Scholarly Antisemitism in Nazi Germany*. Cambridge, MA: Harvard University Press.

Strenski, Ivan. 1987. *Four Theories of Myth in Twentieth Century History: Cassirer, Eliade, Levi Strauss and Malinowski*. London: Macmillan.

Szanton, David L., ed. 2004. *The Politics of Knowledge: Area Studies and the Disciplines*. Berkeley: University of California Press.

Tirosh-Rothschild, Hava. 1991. *Between Worlds: The Life and Thought of Rabbi David ben Judah Messer Leon*. Albany: State University of New York Press.

Tylor, Edward Burnett. 1970a [1958]. *The Origins of Culture*. Intro. Paul Radin. Gloucester, MA: Peter Smith.

———. 1970b [1958]. *Religion in Primitive Culture*. Intro. Paul Radin. Gloucester, MA: Peter Smith.

Wasserstrom, Steven M. 1999. *Religion after Religion: Gershom Scholem, Mircea Eliade, and Henry Corbin at Eranos*. Princeton, NJ: Princeton University Press.

Wiese, Christian. 2005. *Challenging Colonial Discourse: Jewish Studies and Protestant Theology in Wilhelmine Germany*. Leiden: Brill.

Wolff, Jonathan. 2002. *Why Read Marx Today?* Oxford: Oxford University Press.

Wolfson, Elliot R. 2005. *Language, Eros, Being: Kabbalistic Hermeneutics and Poetic Imagination*. New York: Fordham University Press.

———. 2010a. *A Dream Interpreted within a Dream: Oneiropoesis and the Prism of Imagination*. New York: Zone Books.

———. 2010b. "That Old Time Religion." *Azure* 41: 97–108.

Wolfson, Harry, A. 1921. "The Needs of Jewish Scholarship in America." *The Menorah Journal* 7.1: 28–35.

Yerushalmi, Yosef Hayim. 1989. *Zakhor: Jewish History and Jewish Memory*. Seattle: University of Washington Press.

Zunz, Leopold. 1995 [1873]. "On Rabbinical Literature." In Paul Mendes-Flohr and Jehuda Reinharz, eds. *The Jew in the Modern World: A Documentary History*, 2nd ed., 221–223. Oxford and New York: Oxford University Press, 1995.

Index

Made in the USA
Middletown, DE
12 October 2016